A Year of
SEW MUCH FUN

*24 seasonal projects for
the whole family*

By Roz Davies

First published in 2014 by:
The Contemporary Sewing Company Ltd,
Victoria Gardens, Victoria Street,
Windermere, Cumbria, LA23 1AD
www.sewmuchfun.co.uk

Photography: Piero Pierini
Editorial: Emily Ross-Joannou
Design: Margarita Lorenzo
Illustrations: Roz Davies

First Edition
A catalogue record for this book is available from the British Library

ISBN 978-0-9931352-0-0

Printed in the UK
www.thechoirpress.co.uk

*To my lovely daughters
Florence and Georgia
and to all my students*

CONTENTS

INTRODUCTION

Easily recognisable by the pink and purple streaks in her hair, Roz Davies, the owner of Sew Much Fun is typically found in her colourful shop surrounded by pots of buttons, reels of ribbons, squares of felt and bolts of bright contemporary prints. With 30 years of production engineering and design management experience under her belt, two artisan sewing shops to her name and a lifetime of sewing tips to share, Roz not only teaches her customers to make their own clothes, stuffed toys and soft furnishings but also passes on her boundless enthusiasm for her craft. This is her story.

"I was born in Liverpool in 1960 and lived with my mother Ann, father Peter and my older brother Simon. Creativity has always been a big part of my life – as children we would transform our bedrooms into ships using bed sheets for sails or convert our playroom into a restaurant and serve meals made from colourful plasticine.

Although my mother didn't sew herself she loved textiles and always encouraged me to use my hands. I first started experimenting with needle and thread when I was five or six but I really began making things around my tenth birthday when my mother bought me a lovely illustrated book by Jane Chapman called the Girls Book of Sewing. I read it from cover to cover and tried out most of the projects. Sewing drew me in from the very start and I loved how the world seemed to disappear while you were doing it.

At primary school once a week while the boys played football, the girls learnt to hand sew and use old fashioned Singer sewing machines. I think we were one of the last generations to automatically get such a thorough sewing education at school.

When I was 15 my secondary school sewing teacher took the class to a sewing exhibition in the famous bookshop Foyles on Charing Cross Road, which was put on by the embroidery

"Once a week while the boys played football, the girls learnt to hand sew"

department at the London College of Fashion (LCF). It was the first time I'd ever heard of the LCF and the intricacy of the embroidery I saw fired my imagination.

Once I decided I wanted to get into the clothing industry, sewing became my main preoccupation and I spent a lot of time making my own clothes. The style at the time was pretty hippy and I used to turn up to sixth form in handmade long tiered skirts which fell to my ankles with my petticoat showing. I used to finish the outfit off with one of my father's oversized jumpers!

In 1978, I started the 'Clothing Management' course at the LCF, run by the Clothing Institute which trained students up for the fashion industry – one of the largest employers in the UK at the time. It was a four-year business studies course focused on the clothing industry and it was everything I hoped it would be.
I learnt how to make a man's suit, how to use an industrial pattern and how to design. Traditionally the course was meant

Girls Book of Sewing: the guide which sparked off Roz's sewing passion at the age of 10

for the sons and daughters of factory owners so in that way I was unusual as I didn't have a family business to go onto once the course was finished.

After graduating in 1982 I decided to follow the production route and got my first job at the age of 22 as a production engineer for a company based in High Wycombe which produced clothes for Marks & Spencer. Hard to believe today but in those days M&S was at the epicentre of the fashion industry and I worked there for two and a half years. It was an excellent insight into mass production.

I decided to move back to London and over the next decade or so I worked in production engineering and design management for other suppliers to Marks & Spencer including the Tootal Group and Courtaulds Textiles. One of my key achievements was helping to introduce CAD (computer-aided design) into the fashion industry supply chain.

When I got married to Geoffrey in 1992 I was managing a Design Studio with over a 100 people in it – unheard of now in the UK, and we settled down to live in Camden Town. Although Geoff is an accountant he has always been supportive of my creativity and we often joke that he sees life in black and white numbers whilst I see it just in colour!

We had our first daughter Florence Rose (Flo) in September 1993 followed by Georgia Ann (Gee) who arrived 18 months later. In 1996 I decided I wanted greater flexibility in my working week so I set myself up as a freelance consultant specialising in design management. I was fortunate enough to be invited to be the independent Chair of the Product Development Partnership which was a forward thinking organisation promoting co-operation in supply chain technology. I was also approached by the LCF to be an industry representative to improve the quality of the students dissertations and it was enjoyable to get back involved with the College for a few years.

One of the advantages of being freelance is it gives you time to pursue a variety of activities and around 2000 I started to teach my girls to sew when Flo was seven and Gee six. One of my close friends, Carole Davis, heard what we were up to and encouraged me to teach other children and that's how I began running courses.

The sessions started out in church halls and then my living room which we transformed into a workshop with sewing machines, a sewing table and fabric covering every surface. The courses filled up quickly by word of mouth. My girls came along to all courses and became excellent sewers themselves. By the age of nine Flo had made a pair of pyjamas and while Gee struggled with

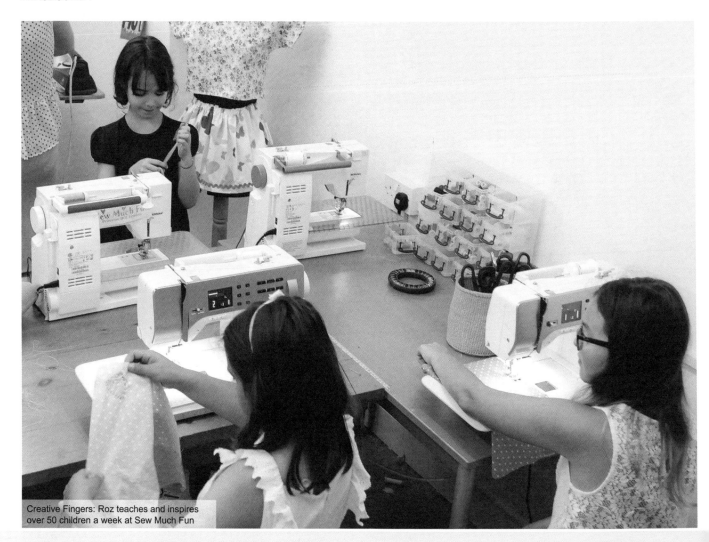
Creative Fingers: Roz teaches and inspires
over 50 children a week at Sew Much Fun

the sewing machine when she was little, she became a brilliant
hand sewer. It was really lovely being able to pass on my skills
and today the girls help run my classes and make things for their
university rooms and gifts for their friends during the holidays.

Also during this time I became involved with a colleague to invent
an electronic tape measure, a project that had serious interest
from companies like Marks & Spencer, Walmart, Hugo Boss and
Benetton. I was fully involved in the design, development and
application of the product but was let down by a dishonest Chief
Executive and the project fell to pieces. We still get asked about
the product today because it is much needed by the industry but
the solution is complex.

Despite feeling incredibly disappointed it was this experience
that drove me to find the bricks and mortar for Sew Much Fun
and run a business entirely on my own. I wanted the shop within
walking distance from home and easy access for the girls to pop
in just in case they had a bad day at school. On December 7th
2007, I opened the doors to Sew Much Fun on Chalcot Road,
Primrose Hill. My aim was to encourage students of all ages to

> *"The sessions started out in church halls and then my living room which we transformed into a workshop"*

take up the creative craft of sewing, to ensure the skill continued
into the next generation and above all to have fun!

I love my shop and think it reflects my personality well – it is
pretty eclectic full of random bits of furniture I have picked up
from junk and antique shops and the shelves are jam-packed
with pots of assorted buttons, ribbons, lace, felt and fleece. I
adore colour and I only stock fabrics I love so the shop is full of
bright prints including a range from Japan.

I wanted to have a friendly fabric shop where people could pop in and ask for advice and I think I have achieved that. I have an open door policy and passers-by are always coming in to browse, ask for tips or seek out the perfect material for a fancy dress outfit.

There were no small sewing shops like mine when I first set up Sew Much Fun and I think the locals thought I was completely mad trying to get it going particularly when the recession hit but we managed to survive and today I think it's fair to say I'm now part of the local community. So many of the local kids start lessons here when they are at primary school and love it so much they continue until they go to university.

For the first few years I ran the business by myself with a few weekly sewing classes and a wide range of commissions including a range of clothes for some unusually shaped toys, personalised cushions, penguins and monsters!

Today I have a wide range of customers – from the nesting pregnant mums and doting grannies to the eager ten year olds. The classes are always small (never more than six adults), and have a relaxed, friendly and encouraging atmosphere. I teach and guide in line with the customer's ability. Some professionals come for a creative outlet, other more advanced sewers come because it gives them a time each week to dedicate to sewing and some simply enjoy sewing in a group.

My experience as a production engineer makes me a unique type of sewing teacher – I naturally want to make things efficiently and am good at finding techniques to help my customers make things more easily, quickly and successfully.

Encouraging the next generation to sew is something I'm incredibly passionate about particularly since children don't automatically get taught it at school anymore. I think it is such an important skill because it helps develop hand-eye coordination, concentration, creativity and dexterity not to mention the enjoyment children get out of creating. All these things help them do well in other subjects at school and I'm always really proud when I hear that some of the sixth-formers I have taught have gone on to study engineering or architecture.

Using your hands is fundamentally good for you and the kids just adore it. Sometimes the children find techniques hard and although my one rule is 'no glue!' I will always find ways to make things easier for them and so they come away with a sense of achievement.

In 2012 I decided it was time to bite the bullet and expand the business. Geoff and I have been spending summers in Windermere in the Lake District for many years and have always planned to retire up there. When we visited a few summers ago

"Encouraging the next generation to sew is something I'm incredibly passionate about"

we decided it would be the perfect location for a new shop. We discovered a really cute wooden chalet, surrounded by parkland, with a lovely row of windows down one side giving it lots of natural light and making it a great place to work and create. I immediately fell in love with it. When the sale went through in February 2013 our goal was to restore this charming hut to its former glory when it belonged to the local railway in Victoria Gardens.

In July 2013 we opened Sew Much Fun number two. The set-up and design of the shop is very similar to the Primrose Hill branch with a fabric shop and sewing courses and the signature pink wall. We've had a wonderful response so far from local sewers and I'm keen to build up a customer base and the courses we offer over the coming years.

I love coming to work every day. I get great satisfaction from sharing my knowledge and seeing how happy it makes people to learn a new skill which is why I wanted to write this book."

How to use A Year of Sew Much Fun

This book has a year's worth of projects for you to enjoy. During the first six months the projects get progressively harder and each chapter introduces you to new techniques so you will grow in confidence. The illustrated instructions should be used alongside the techniques section at the back of the book showing you how to copy off the patterns, cut out, hand and machine sew. There are many other sewing techniques to learn but I will save them for another book!

I have included my sewing machine practice sheet which is aimed at absolute beginners and many of the very popular projects we make at Sew Much Fun. The projects are for the whole family and the book can be shared and used by all ages. Successful sewing is about accuracy but you can have great fun and lots of personal satisfaction whilst you learn this craft.

I do hope you enjoy this book, and please send me pictures of what you make.

Happy Sewing

MY SEWING BOX

You can easily start your sewing career with just a needle and thread, a pair of sharp scissors and some felt. But, if you want to progress you need to consider the contents of your sewing box. Sewing tools and equipment can be collected over time and the more expensive ones can make great birthday and Christmas presents. In this chapter I will tell you what we use in the workshops at Sew Much Fun to support our sewing creativity.

SEWING MACHINES

To maximize your sewing time you really do need a sewing machine and I often get asked about which machine to buy. Experts all have their favourites and my preferred make is Bernina with an automatic buttonhole facility and solid feet replacing the clip on feet, but I am very aware they don't come cheap! My advice is to decide on your budget and when purchasing think about how you might get support servicing or fixing the machine and then remember 'you get what you pay

for'! Cheaper machines will have their limitations so if you want to hem your jeans make sure the sewing machine specification will allow you to do this. Always consider an old machine your Great Aunt has in the attic and that a sewing machine could last you for 25 years not the standard 18 months all our other modern gadgets last for!

CUTTING AND MEASURING EQUIPMENT

I have a variety of measuring tools mainly with cms and inches on. Steel rulers of different lengths and widths: 100 cm, 60 cm and 30 cm; and a good quality tape measure. I also find a non-slip 12" x 6" quilting ruler useful for general sewing but a rotary knife and cutting mat are essential for cutting patchwork. I am very precious about my sharp fabric scissors and again I have a variety of sizes and identify them with a ribbon tie so they must not be used for anything but fabric. You also need scissors for cutting paper and card. Pinking shears are nice to have but difficult to keep sharp so I now advise buying a rotary knife with a pinking blade.

THREADS AND BOBBINS

When your sewing progresses you will start to collect threads. I like Gutermann threads but I mainly use a 'sew all' thread because of their broad use. You can get all sorts of threads for all sorts of projects; cotton, linen, recycled and embroidery – the list is endless but to keep it simple I'd recommend 'sew all' for the projects in this book. To help manage reel and bobbin colour sets for the machine I suggest you purchase at least a dozen extra bobbins.

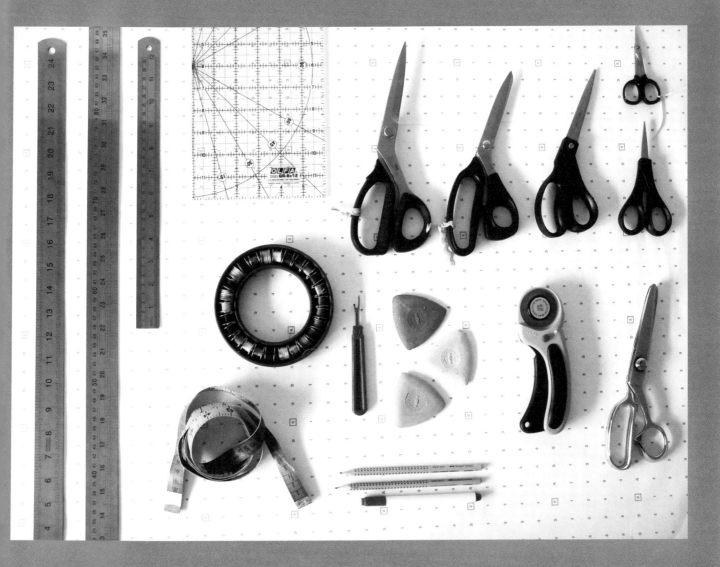

PINS AND NEEDLES

I am a complete sucker for pretty pins and while they are not the finest you can buy, they will work perfectly well for all the projects in this book and the bobble heads show up in the fleece and on the floor. If I am ever doing fine work then I would always make sure my needles and pins were as fine as they needed to be. I rarely sew with a thimble but I do have a silver one that is a perfect fit.

It is also important to have a range of sewing machine needles to suit the project you are doing. The finer they are the lower the number and all our projects were sewn on a 90 which is available in a standard assorted pack but you can get fine, heavy, ballpoint needles for knitted fabric and leather needles. Safety pins in various sizes are useful for threading through ribbons and rope and an 'unpicker' is every sewers friend!

MARKING TOOLS

I use tailor's chalk all the time for marking patterns and lines on the wrong side of the fabric and I also use pencils for fabric and paper so a good pencil sharpener is essential. I make seam allowance gauges with a scrap of paper and a ruler and when doing embroidery I use an invisible pen.

CREATIVE PARAPHERNALIA

To develop all my design ideas I have to have pattern paper which is conveniently marked with 2 cm squares and thin enough for tracing through. To expand on these ideas I often use a calico fabric, which is a natural un-dyed cotton to make up my first samples. This allows experimentation at low cost and you can also draw on it to clearly identify necessary alterations. A pattern curve is also nice to have but not essential.

You cannot get away from the fact that technical sewing has a strong mathematical element. You are often dealing in half size, quarter size and π for calculations so a calculator is a must!

STARTING TO SEW

This section is for complete beginners who are new to the sewing machine. It will help you understand basic sewing machine terminology, encourage you to refer to your sewing machine manual and give you a few sewing machine exercises to get you used to handling a machine.

SEWING MACHINE TERMINOLOGY

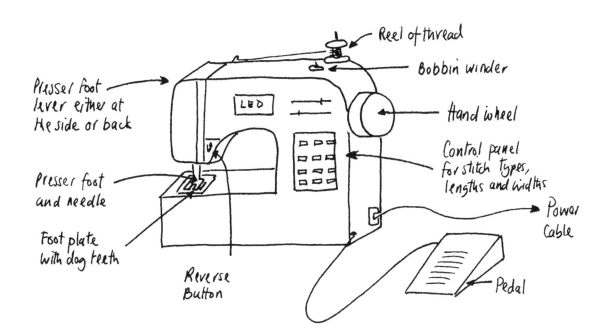

Reel of thread

Bobbin winder

Hand wheel

Control panel for stitch types, lengths and widths

Power Cable

Pedal

Reverse Button

Foot plate with dog teeth

Presser foot and needle

Presser foot lever either at the side or back

LED

ROZ'S TIP

Sometimes when you finish your sewing, it can be difficult to draw out your thread and you end up with four threads instead of the normal two. Don't worry, nothing is broken you just need to wind your needle up to the top of its cycle and you will see that it will come out smoothly.

WINDING A BOBBIN AND THREADING A MACHINE

Your sewing machine manual will help you with this but I suggest you put an hour or two aside to practice before you leap into any sewing project.

SEWING MACHINE EXERCISES
Copy the sewing practice sheet onto some paper. Use this as a guide to start learning how to control your machine.

SEWING A STRAIGHT LINE
To sew a straight stitch you should use a stitch length of 2.5 mm for sewing.

When sewing on your sheet with your machine threaded, follow down one of the straight lines to begin with, using a straight stitch. Clamp the paper firmly in position by letting down your presser foot lever and press the pedal with your foot to move the needle up and down and move the paper along with the dog teeth which are situated beneath the presser foot. You should not have to pull or push the paper through with your hands but you will have to guide the paper with light fingers to keep it on the line. When the row is finished, unclamp the paper by lifting the presser foot lever up, draw the thread out and cut either with sissors or with a cutter on the machine. Do a couple more lines. Please remember to keep your fingers well away from the needle because the machine is powerful enough to stitch into a finger.

SEWING A ZIGZAG LINE
To sew a zigzag stitch you should use a stitch width of 3 mm and a stitch length of 1.5 mm.

Repeat the same exercise with a zigzag stitch.

SECURING YOUR SEAM WITH A BACKSTITCH
Repeat again with a straight stitch. This time after you have sewn the first five stitches you should press the reverse button and whilst keeping it pressed, stitch five stitches backwards. This process is called 'back stitching' and you use it at the beginning and end of any construction seam to secure your stitching. It is assumed that you will automatically do this at the start and finish of your seam, for all the projects in this book.

SEWING A CORNER
Once you have mastered the above, (the younger you are the longer it will take!) think about sewing the angled lines. This is to help you learn to manipulate. With a straight stitch, sew up to the first turn and wind your needle with your hand wheel into the paper to hold it firmly. Then lift up the presser foot with your presser foot lever and swing the paper around until the new sewing line is at the right angle for sewing. Put the presser foot down and sew to the next turn and repeat. This starts to teach you how to maneuver with the sewing machine and how to create perfect corners.

Repeat this exercise using just a straight stitch on all the other shapes including your 'back stitch'. Once complete you are well on your way to having the machine sewing skills for completing the first project.

Good Luck!

SEWING MACHINE PRACTICE SHEET

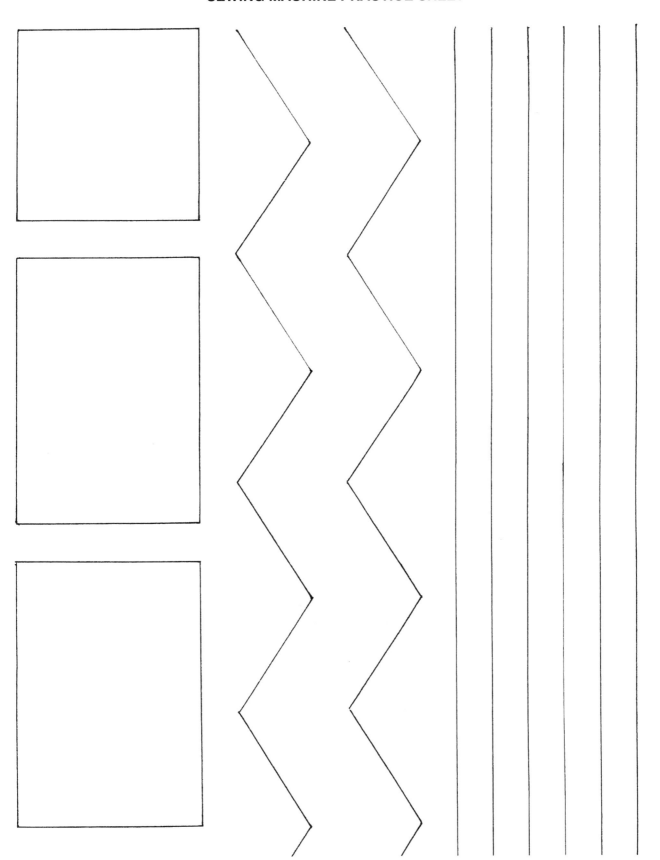

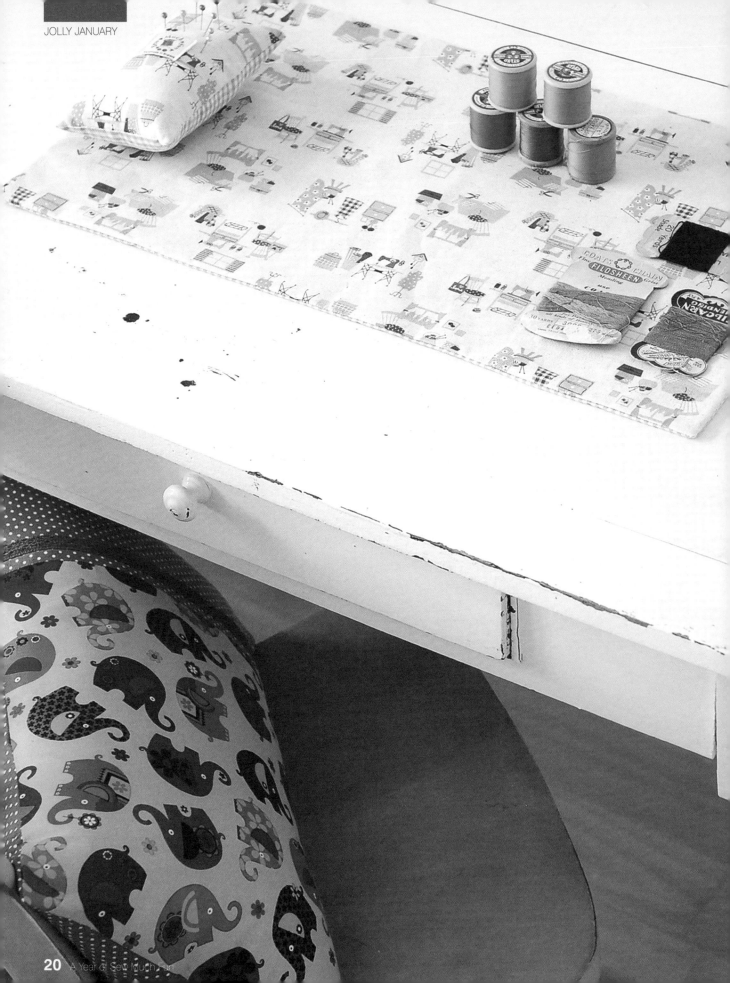

JOLLY JANUARY

Let's learn to sew

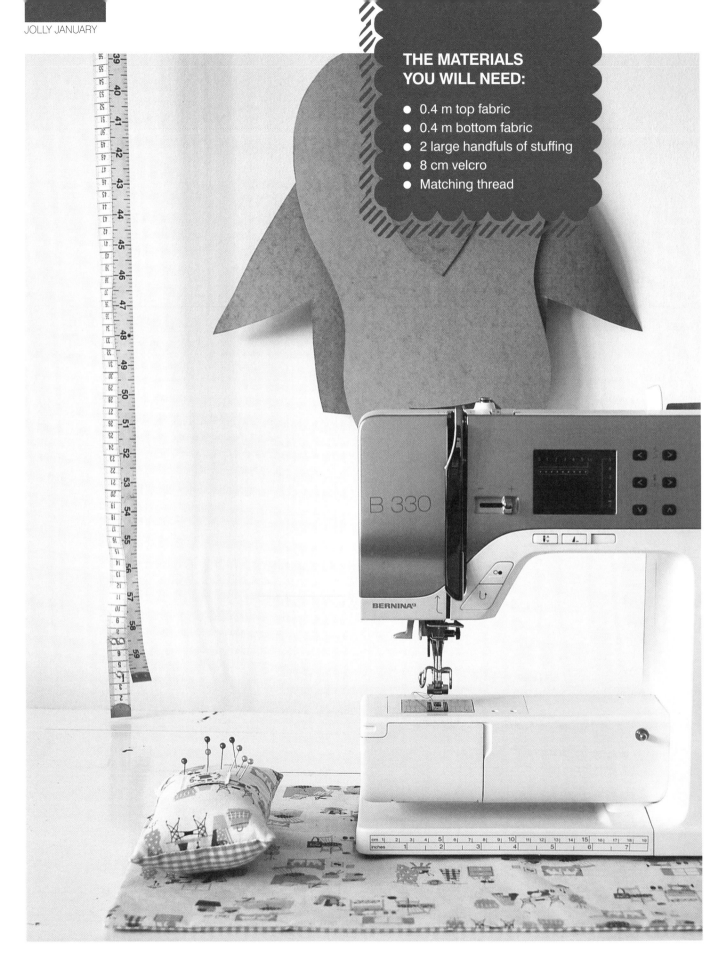

THE MATERIALS YOU WILL NEED:

- 0.4 m top fabric
- 0.4 m bottom fabric
- 2 large handfuls of stuffing
- 8 cm velcro
- Matching thread

Machine Mat and Pin Cushion

This project introduces you to sewing straight, managing corners and getting into the habit of backstitching to secure your sewing. Without the pin cushion the same technique makes a great table mat.

CUTTING INSTRUCTIONS
HOW TO MAKE IT

1 Enlarge the pattern for the mat by three to measure 55 cm x 33 cm and the pin cushion pattern piece, to measure 12 cm x 18 cm. Use these patterns to cut a top and bottom for each item from the two fabrics.

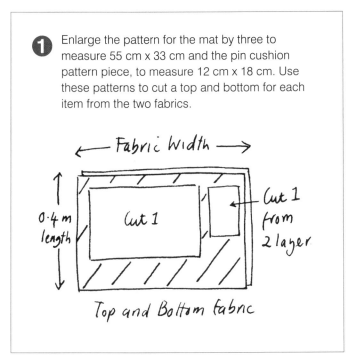

2 Take the top fabric of the mat right side facing up and place the soft side of the velcro 12.5 cm from the top and 6cm in from the side, sew in place.

6 Snip off excess fabric at the corners and turn the mat and pin cushion through to the right side. Press flat.

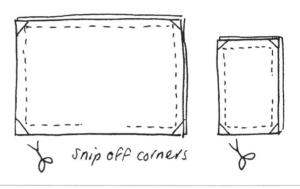

snip off corners

3 Take the bottom half of the pin cushion right side facing up and place the spiky side of the velcro 5 cm down from the top and in from the side and sew in place.

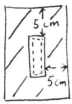

Sew on Velcro to bottom fabric

5 cm
5 cm

7 Hand sew the gap in the mat using a slip stitch. Stuff the pin cushion as tight as you can and hand sew the gap up using a slip stitch. It helps if you pin the gap together first.

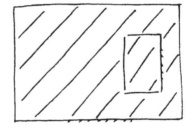

Turn through, stuff pincushion Sew up gaps with slip stitch

4 Taking the top and bottom of the mat place right sides together and pin together. Sew around using a 1 cm seam allowance. Leave a gap in the middle of the long edge to turn through.

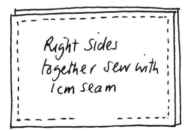

Right sides together sew with 1cm seam

8 Place the pin cushion velcro onto the mat velcro and hey presto you have a very useful sewing mat and removable pin cushion.

5 Repeat for the pin cushion remembering to place the right sides together.

Right sides together sew with 1cm seam

ROZ'S TIP

To help you to stitch correctly you can always draw a line with a pencil or a piece of tailor's chalk along the seam line that you should be sewing. Only do this when you are sewing on the wrong side of your fabric.

Enlarge Patterns by 3 or 300%

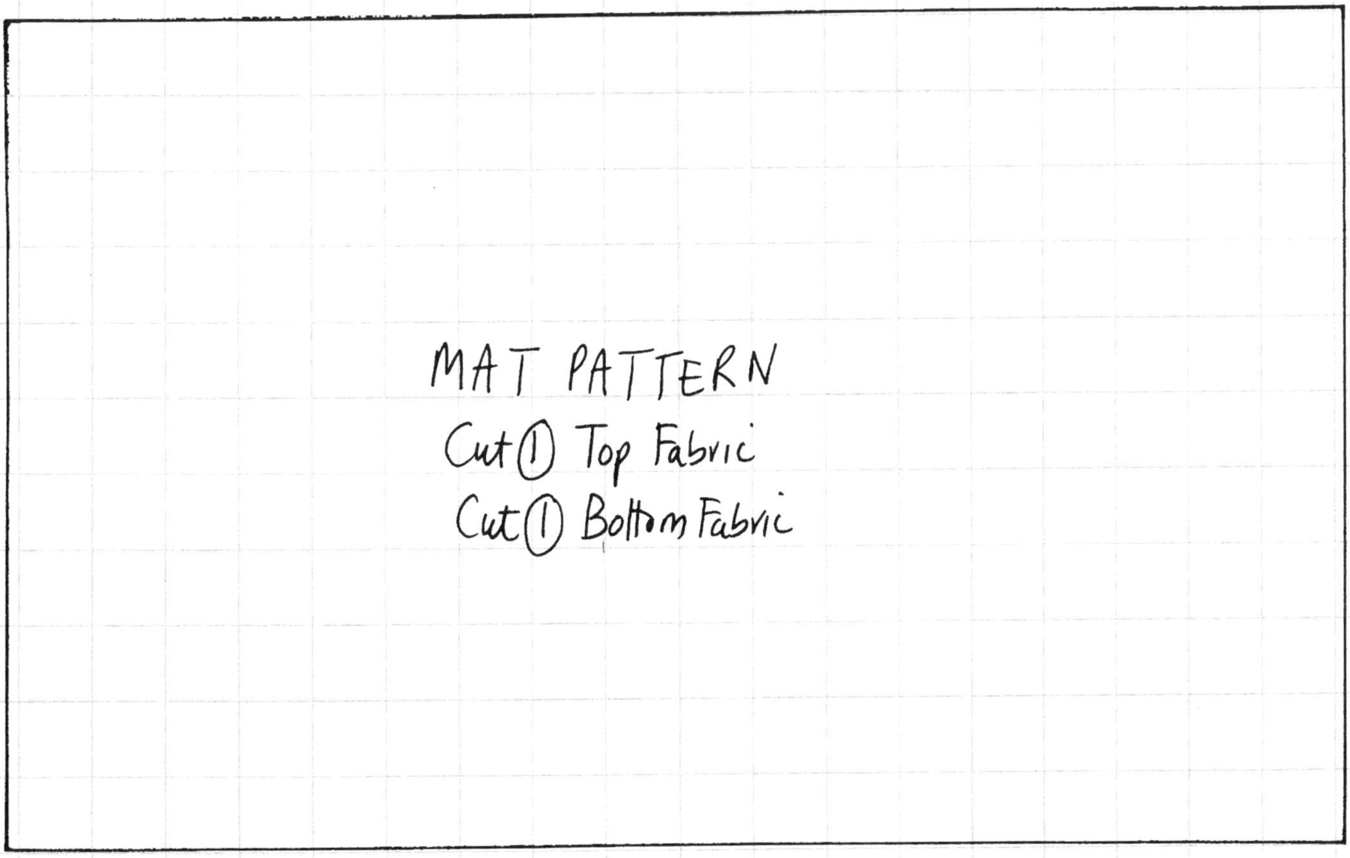

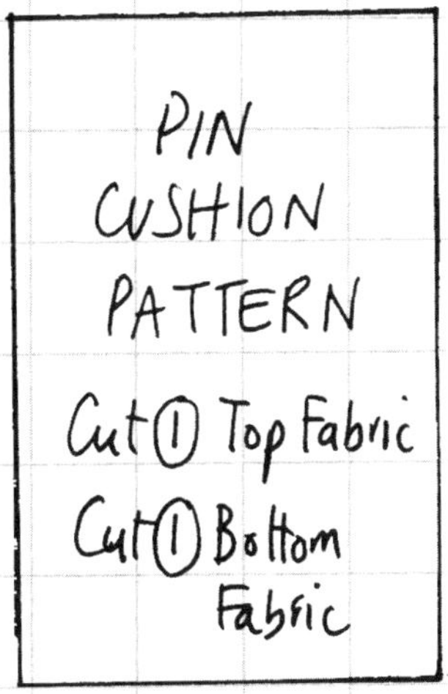

MAT PATTERN
Cut ① Top Fabric
Cut ① Bottom Fabric

PIN
CUSHION
PATTERN
Cut ① Top Fabric
Cut ① Bottom Fabric

THE MATERIALS YOU WILL NEED:

- 0.4 m front fabric
- 0.4 m contrast and back fabric
- 0.4 m of cushion lining fabric (do not iron)
- 500 g stuffing
- 0.4 m of co-ordinating trim
- Matching thread

Creative Cushion

This cushion for your sewing seat is simple to make and gives you the chance to be creative with your fabric choice. The design can also be used to make cushions for around the house.

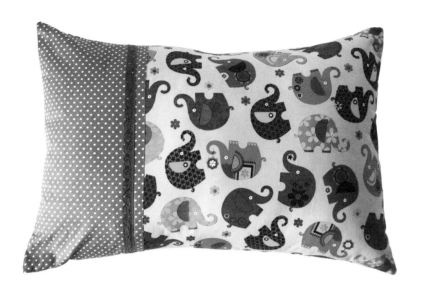

ROZ'S TIP

To get professional corners always trim off the excess fabric around the corner and turn through carefully with your fingers.

CUTTING INSTRUCTIONS
HOW TO MAKE IT

1

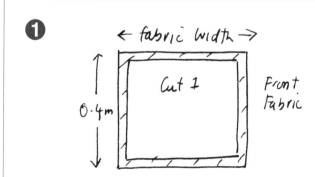

Enlarge the cushion lining pattern by three to measure 50 cm x 33 cm. Cut two out of the cushion lining fabric.

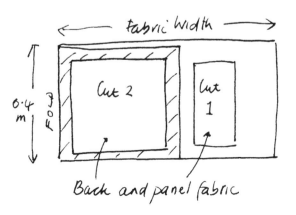

Enlarge the cushion pad pattern by three to measure 33 cm x 33 cm and the cushion panel to measure 19 cm x 33 cm. Using the cushion pattern, cut one in the front fabric and two in the contrast fabric. Cut one cushion panel in the contrast fabric.

2 Take the front fabric and the contrast panel, right sides together and sew with a 1 cm seam allowance. Press flat.

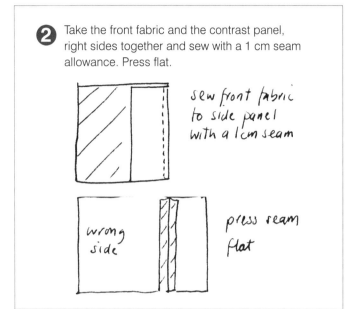

sew front fabric to side panel with a 1cm seam

wrong side

press seam flat

3 Place the trim parallel to the seam either on the contrast fabric or the front fabric then pin and sew in place.

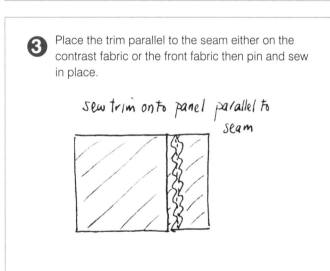

sew trim onto panel parallel to seam

4 Take the two contrast cushion pieces and to make the back opening, neaten one edge on each side using a 1 cm double-folded hem.

sew a double seam on opening edge of back fabric

5 With right sides together of the front and the two backs of the cushion sew all around using a 1 cm seam allowance. Snip corners, turn through the gap at the back of the cushion then press.

right sides together sew 1cm all around

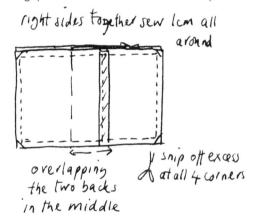

overlapping the two backs in the middle

snip off excess at all 4 corners

6 Take the cushion lining pieces and sew together using a 1 cm seam allowance and leaving a gap for the stuffing. Snip corners, turn through, stuff and hand sew the gap with a slip stitch.

sew lining together with 1cm seam

snip all corners

7 Place the cushion pad into cushion cover and now you have your lovely creative cushion. This can be repeated in all sorts of colour combinations and alternative trims.

Enlarge Patterns by 3 or 300%

CUSHION PATTERN
Cut ① Front Fabric
Cut ② Contrast / Back Fabric

CUSHION PANEL
PATTERN
Cut ① Contrast
Fabric

CUSHION PAD PATTERN
Cut ② Cushion lining

FOND FEBRUARY

Keep your love warm

THE MATERIALS YOU WILL NEED:

- Scraps of cotton fabric for the top
- Scraps of fleece for the bottom
- Stuffing
- Squeaker
- Matching thread

Squeaky Bone

At this time of year we need gifts for those we love – even the canine sort! Using fabric scraps, the bone introduces you to curves without any pressure of them having to be perfect. It also teaches you how to sew with two different types of fabric.

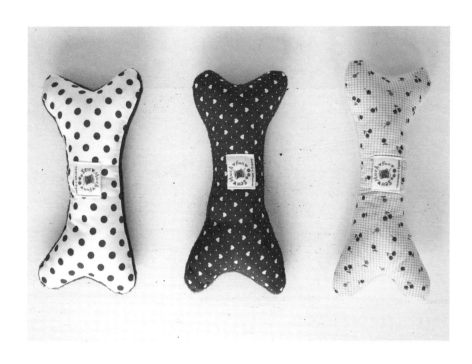

CUTTING INSTRUCTIONS
HOW TO MAKE IT

1 Copy the bone pattern and use this pattern to cut out the top fabric.

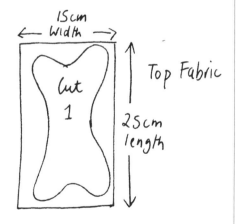

15cm
← Width →

Cut 1

Top Fabric

25cm length

Find a piece of scrap fleece fabric measuring 15 cm x 25 cm so your cut out bone can fit on it.

2 With right sides together place the top fabric onto the fleece fabric. Sew around the shape with a foot width seam allowance and a gap on one side of the middle for turning through and stuffing.

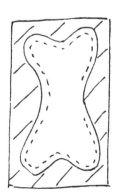

right sides together sew with a foot width seam

3 Trim off the excess fleece and snip around the curves.

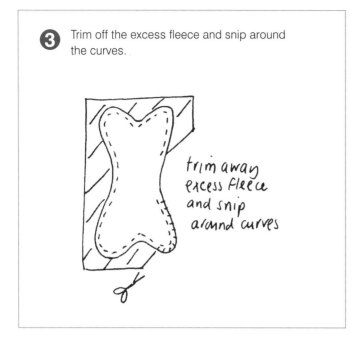

trim away excess fleece and snip around curves

4 Turn through and stuff the bone adding the squeaker in the middle when you are finished. Hand sew the gap with a slip stitch.

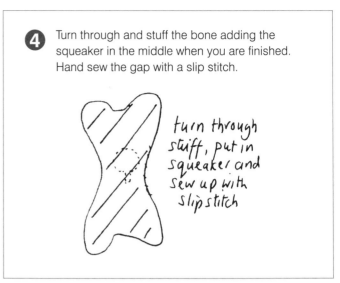

turn through stuff, put in squeaker and sew up with slip stitch

ROZ'S TIP

If you are making an intricate shape, cut one side of your fabric accurately to the shape and cut a rectangle on the other side that easily covers your shape. Sew with right sides together from the side with the intricate shape using the edge as a guide and then cut off the excess fabric afterwards.

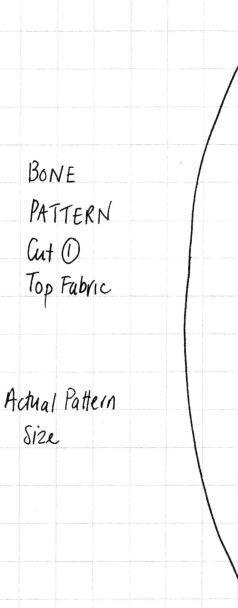

BONE
PATTERN
Cut ①
Top Fabric

Actual Pattern
Size

ROZ'S TIP

It is much easier to cut out patchwork shapes using imperial inches.

THE MATERIALS YOU WILL NEED:

- Scraps of cotton fabric for the fr●
- 25 cm x 25 cm contrast or co-ordinating fabric for the back
- A couple of large handfuls of stu
- Loose lavender
- Matching thread

Patchwork Lavender Heart

This patchwork heart gets your creative juices flowing by selecting a variety of fabrics that blend well together, whilst sewing more curves and developing your rotary cutting skills.

CUTTING INSTRUCTIONS
HOW TO MAKE IT

1 Cut out 14 squares – 6.4 cm (2 1/2") each. Copy the heart pattern on the fold and use this pattern to cut out the fabric back.

Cut 1
Bottom Fabric

25cm square

2.5" square

assorted scrap fabric

x 14

2 Sew the squares together using a foot width seam allowance in three rows of four and one row of two. Then sew the rows together with the same seam allowance.

right sides together sew. with a foot width seam

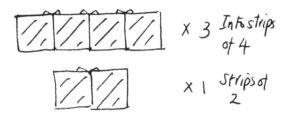

x 3 Into strips of 4

x 1 Strips of 2

Then sew the strips together to build up the patchwork

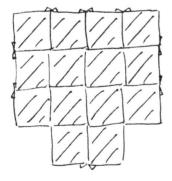

3 With right sides together place the back fabric cut out in a heart shape onto the patchwork and sew around with a foot width seam allowance and a gap in one of the straighter sides.

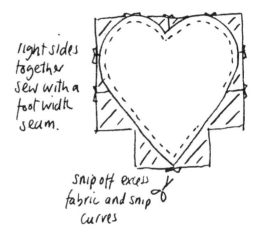

right sides together sew with a foot width seam.

snip off excess fabric and snip curves

4 Trim off the excess patchwork, snip around the curves and turn through.

5 Stuff carefully into all corners and then place a handful of lavender in the middle. Don't be too liberal with the lavender or you will keep the recipient awake all night!

Turn through stuff, add lavender and slip stitch closed

6 Hand sew closed with a slip stitch.

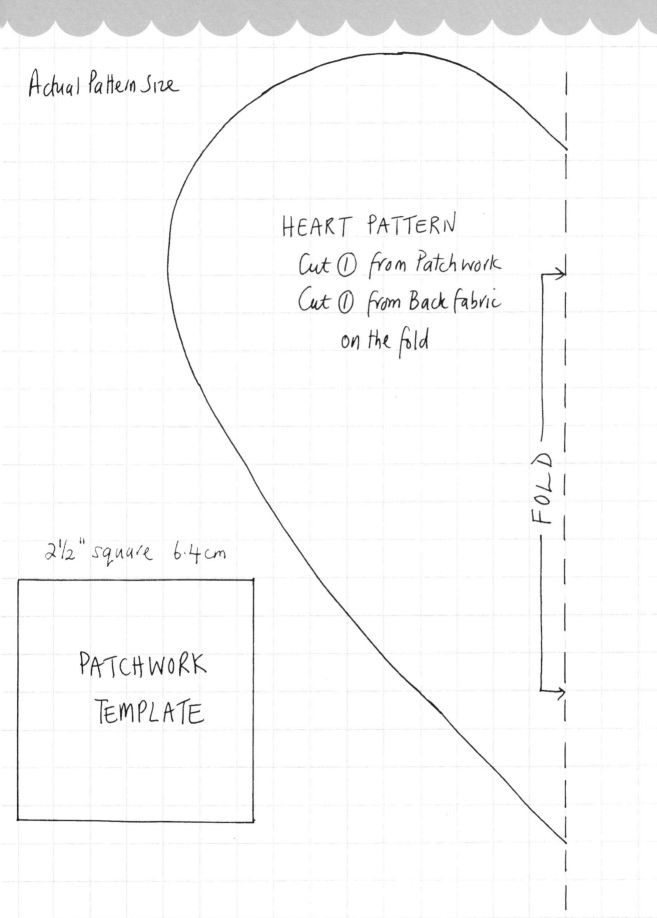

Actual Pattern Size

HEART PATTERN
Cut ① from Patchwork
Cut ① from Back fabric
on the fold

FOLD

2½" square 6.4 cm

PATCHWORK
TEMPLATE

MESSY MARCH

Be spick and span

THE MATERIALS YOU WILL NEED:
To make an Adult's apron
- 1 m of calico fabric
- 0.25 m of the pocket fabric
- 30 cm square of grey washable felt
- 30 cm square of red washable felt
- 30 cm square of toffee washable felt
- 1.80 m of 4 cm wide tape/webbing
- Matching thread

Cooking Apron

With spring cleaning in the air an apron is a must. This design is a Sew Much Fun favourite and my customers often add more appliqué including names, hearts and cakes. This project also reinforces your ability to sew straight and accurately.

CUTTING INSTRUCTIONS
HOW TO MAKE IT

1 Enlarge the apron pattern by four on the fold so the length is 92 cm and the half width is 34 cm. Use this pattern to cut out the apron on the folded piece of calico.

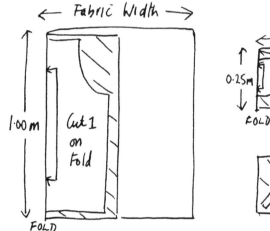

Enlarge the apron pocket pattern by four so the depth is 21 cm and the half width is 16 cm. Use this pattern to cut out the pocket on a folded piece of the pocket fabric.

Copy the cooking utensils patterns and cut them out of the felt. Use grey for the whisk, toffee for the spoon and spatula handle and red for the spatula itself.

2 Measure 41 cms down the apron and place the bottom end of the spatula, whisk and wooden spoon along that line at your preferred angle. Pin the items in place and sew on using an edge stitch. Use the same colour thread as the apron.

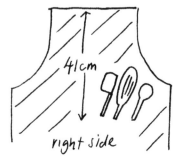

3 Hem the straight edge of the pocket with a 1 cm double-folded hem. Then sew a line with a 1 cm seam allowance all the way around the curved edge. Snip in around the curves.

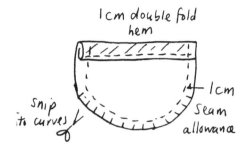

1cm double fold hem

snip to curves

1cm seam allowance

4 Using the stitched line, fold the edge of the pocket towards the wrong side of the fabric producing a really nice curved even edge. Place the pocket centrally on the apron 39 cm down from the top. Pin and sew in place with an edge stitch. Then sew a line down the centre of the pocket to stop it from gaping open.

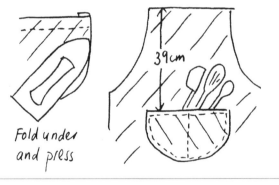

39cm

Fold under and press

5 Neaten the curves with a 1 cm double-folded hem. Press the apron flat first, then pin and sew. Next sew the same hem along the top, sides and bottom of the apron.

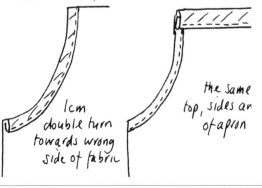

1cm double turn towards wrong side of fabric

the same top, sides an of apron

6 Cut off 58 cm of tape/webbing for your neck strap. With the right side of your apron upper most, fold under 2 cm of the end of the strap and place on the top right hand side of your apron. Pin in place. Making sure you do not put a twist in the strap, fold under 2 cm the other end and place it on the top left hand side of your apron.

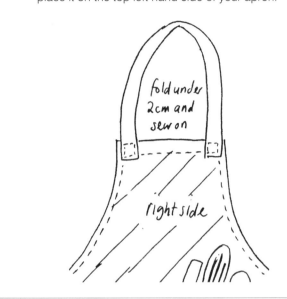

fold under 2cm and sew on

right side

7 Cut the remaining tape/webbing in two and attach to the sides of the apron using the same method explained in the previous step, To stop the straps from fraying at the ends, neaten with a 1 cm double fold.

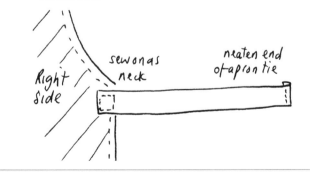

Right side

sew on as neck

neaten end of apron tie

ROZ'S TIP

The apron pattern is a standard shape so you can enlarge it by three and get a junior apron, by two and get an infant's apron or leave it as it is and get a dolls apron! Just remember to re-adjust the size of the appliqué as well.

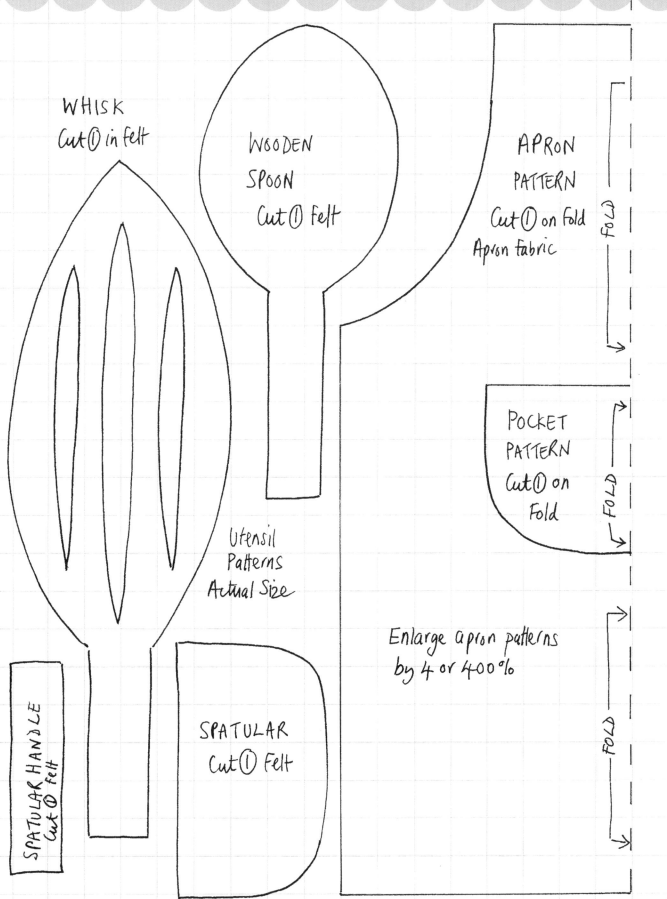

WHISK
Cut ① in felt

WOODEN
SPOON
Cut ① Felt

APRON
PATTERN
Cut ① on Fold
Apron Fabric

FOLD

Utensil
Patterns
Actual Size

POCKET
PATTERN
Cut ① on
Fold

FOLD

Enlarge apron patterns
by 4 or 400%

SPATULAR HANDLE
Cut ② Felt

SPATULAR
Cut ① Felt

FOLD

**THE MATERIALS
YOU WILL NEED:**
(For two drawstring bags)
- 0.40 m of bag fabric
- 0.10 m of knicker fabric
- 0.10 m of fusible interlining
- 0.40 m of frilly trim
- 2 colours of washable felt
- 2.80 m ribbon 1 cm wide
- Matching thread for bag fabric
- Matching thread for knicker fabric
- Matching thread for lettering

Drawstring Bag

A decorated drawstring bag is included in all my beginner classes, a simple project that introduces you to sewing channels, which you can repeat at home in various sizes. This design was inspired by one of my regular Wednesday night students – thank you Cristina!

CUTTING INSTRUCTIONS
HOW TO MAKE IT

1 Enlarge the drawstring bag pattern by two on the fold so the length is 40 cms and the width is 35 cms. Using this pattern cut two of the bag pattern. Repeat for the second bag. Make sure you make a snip in on each of the long sides 5 cm from the top, 1 cm deep.

Copy the knicker pattern. Prepare the knicker fabric for appliqué by ironing on interlining to the back of it in a big enough piece for the appliqué design.

Then using the pattern, cut out the knickers, one for each bag. Copy the letters and use as templates for cutting the letters from felt. WASH for one bag WEAR for the other. Felt does not require interlining because it does not fray.

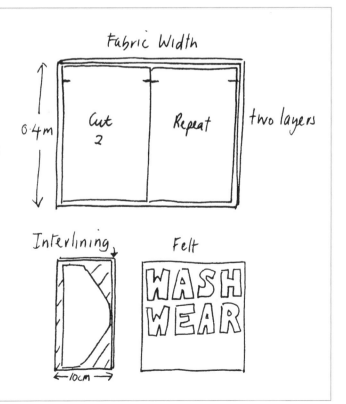

② Place the knickers centrally on the bag front 10 cms up from the bottom of the bag. Sew in place using a zigzag stitch where you have most of the stitch on the knicker. Sew in an extra line to create the knicker line. Highlight this line with contrasting coloured thread using a straight stitch.

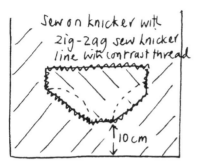

③ Tucking under each end of the frilly trim, sew onto the top of the knickers. Repeat last two steps for the second bag.

④ Place the letters underneath the knickers in a slight curve and sew them on using matching thread with an edge stitch. Repeat for the second bag.

ROZ'S TIP

It is crucial to back fabric that frays with either interlining or Bondaweb for appliqué. I prefer interlining as it gives a softer finish.

⑤ Press the 5 cms turning towards the wrong side of the fabric. Sew them down through the centre. This seam neatens the end of the channel. Again repeat for second bag.

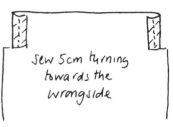

⑥ Along the top edge of both sides of the bag make a 1 cm double-folded hem to create a channel. Repeat for second bag.

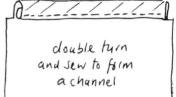

⑦ With right sides of the drawstring bag together, line up the channels at the top and sew a 1 cm seam allowance all the way around the bag.

Snip off excess fabric at the bottom corners and then zigzag this seam to neaten the edges. Repeat for second bag.

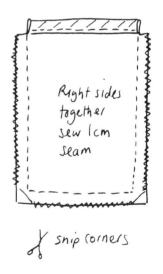

⑧ Turn the drawstring bag through to the right side. Cut your ribbon into lengths of 70 cms. Using a safety pin attached to one end of the ribbon, thread the ribbon through both channels and tie both ribbons together with a simple knot. Repeat this from the other side. This allows you to tighten your bag from both sides. Repeat for second bag.

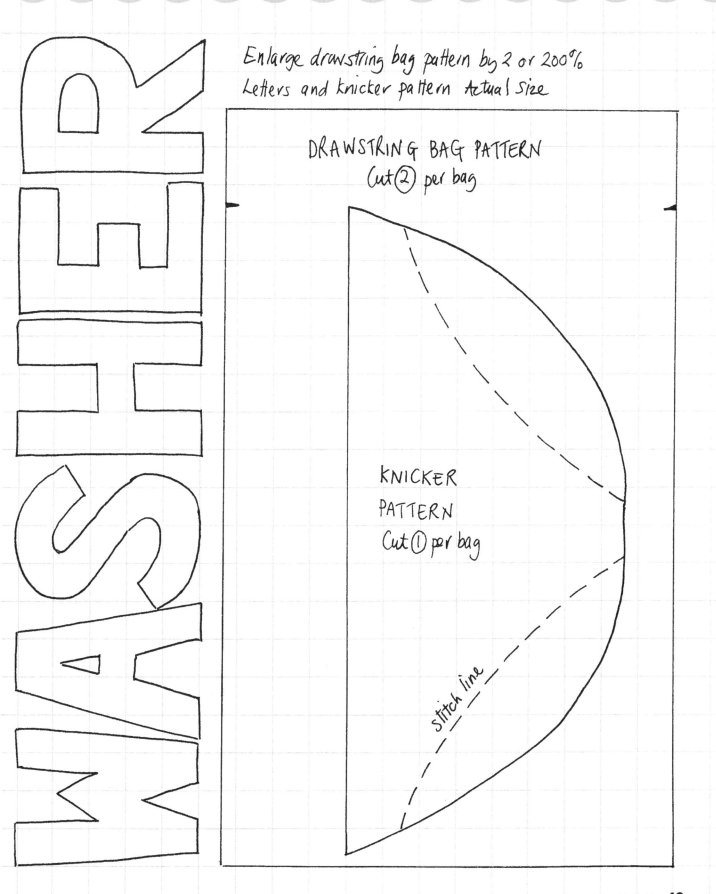

Enlarge drawstring bag pattern by 2 or 200%
Letters and knicker pattern Actual Size

DRAWSTRING BAG PATTERN
Cut ② per bag

KNICKER
PATTERN
Cut ① per bag

stitch line

ADORNED APRIL

Eggcellent decorations

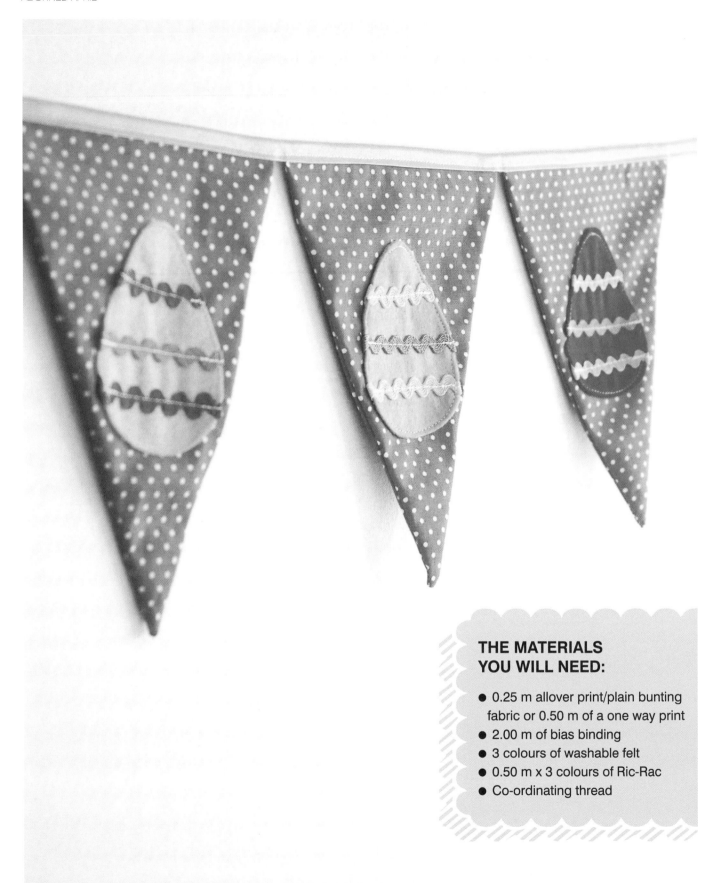

THE MATERIALS
YOU WILL NEED:

- 0.25 m allover print/plain bunting
  fabric or 0.50 m of a one way print
- 2.00 m of bias binding
- 3 colours of washable felt
- 0.50 m x 3 colours of Ric-Rac
- Co-ordinating thread

Easter Bunting

Hanging fabric bunting to mark special occasions has become a popular trend and not only does it look great but it is easy to store and reuse. In this project you will learn how to make your own Easter bunting. The key to success with making bunting is to establish a good pattern shape and flag position accompanied by a quality finish on the binding, which is all clearly explained.

CUTTING INSTRUCTIONS
HOW TO MAKE IT

1. Copy the bunting pattern and cut 10 flags out of your bunting fabric. If your fabric is an allover print you can butt them up to one another but if it is a one way print you must cut them all in the same direction.

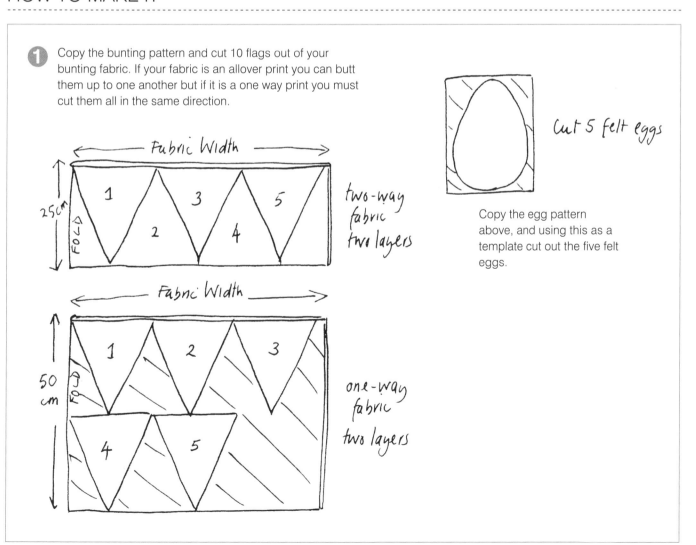

Copy the egg pattern above, and using this as a template cut out the five felt eggs.

2 Decorate the five eggs with the Ric-Rac by sewing down the middle of your Ric-Rac. Make sure you leave some Ric-Rac sticking out each end so you can tuck it under and make it neat when you sew the eggs on the bunting. Place the egg centrally onto the bunting flag, 4 cm down from the top. Sew on using an edge stitch. Repeat for the other four eggs.

decorate eggs with ric-rac

place centrally and sew on. with edge stitch

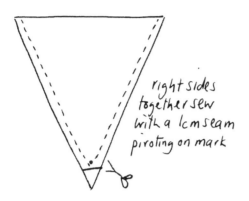

right sides together sew with a 1cm seam pivoting on mark

With right sides together sew the two long sides of the bunting with a foot width seam allowance. To make it easier to get the point right make a pencil mark at the bottom of the flag to turn your stitching on. Snip off excess fabric at point and turn through. Repeat four times and press.

3 Line up your bunting in your preferred order. Start 50 cms along the bias binding (length for tying it up), open up the bias binding and pin onto the back of the bunting flag, lining up all cut edges. Sew along the crease line of the bias binding.

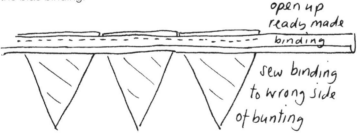

open up ready made binding

sew binding to wrong side of bunting

N.B check your bunting is going in the right direction on the front

4 Then flip over the bias binding onto the front of the bunting flag and pin in place so it wraps over the top edge of the flag. Fold the rest of the bias in two, trapping all the raw edges inside.

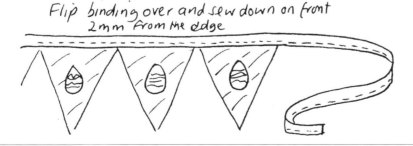

Flip binding over and sew down on front 2mm from the edge

5 Start your sewing at the very end of the bias tape, tucking in the ends. Stitch about 2 mm in from the edge all the way along the bias binding.

ROZ'S TIP

Ric-Rac is a wonderful trim. Easy to sew on straight down the middle and also loves going around curves. But it does fray so always trap the ends in.

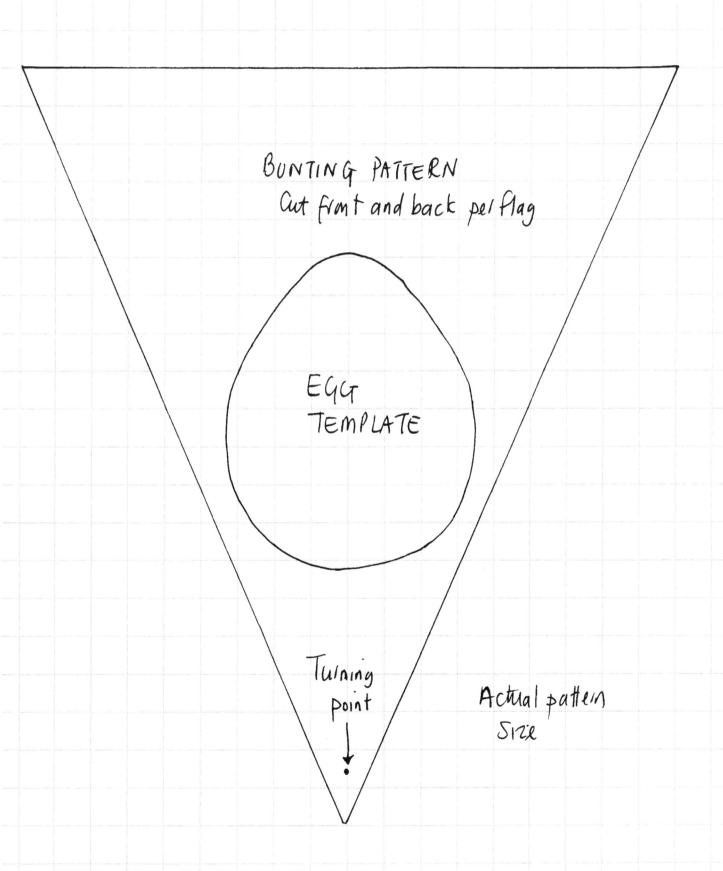

BUNTING PATTERN
Cut front and back per flag

EGG
TEMPLATE

Turning
Point

Actual pattern
Size

THE MATERIALS YOU WILL NEED:

To make a small rabbit
- 30 cm x 25 cm cotton print for the front
- 30 cm x 25 cm fleece for the back
- Scraps of white, pink and eye-coloured felt
- 1 large handful stuffing
- Matching thread

To make a large rabbit
- 60 cm x 50 cm cotton print for the front
- 60 cm x 50 cm fleece for the back
- Scraps of white and pink felt
- Large buttons for eyes
- 500 g of Stuffing
- Matching thread

Bunnies

These huggable bunnies are a great favourite for children of all ages. Originally designed as a toy for infants to grab hold of a leg, arm or ear, this pattern works big or small and just could not be left out of this book!

CUTTING INSTRUCTIONS
HOW TO MAKE IT

1 Copy the rabbit pattern on the fold for the little rabbit. Enlarge by two for the large rabbit. Cut out the cotton print fabric for the front on the fold. Copy out the patterns for the eyes and nose and cut them out of felt.

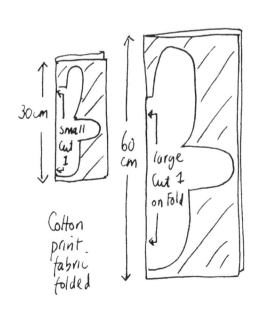

ROZ'S TIP

Remember to snip in all corners and curves to release seam allowances and achieve a quality finish.

2 Using a simple running stitch hand sew on the eyes and the nose. On the large rabbit sew on buttons for the coloured part of the eyes.

hand sew on the eyes and nose

3 With right sides together place the cotton print onto the fleece and sew around the shape with a foot width seam allowance and a gap on one side of the leg.

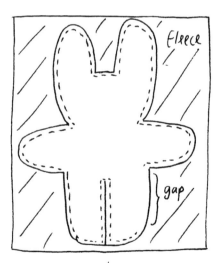

Fleece

gap

right sides together sew around rabbit with a foot width seam

4 Trim off the excess fleece and snip around the curves.

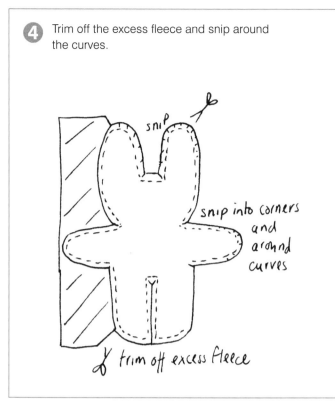

snip

snip into corners and around curves

trim off excess fleece

5 Turn through and stuff the rabbit. Stuffing down the ears, arms and legs takes some time – in fact it's the hardest part of this project!

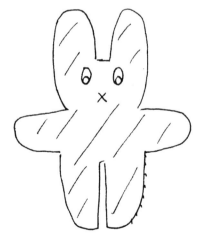

6 Hand sew closed with a slip stitch.

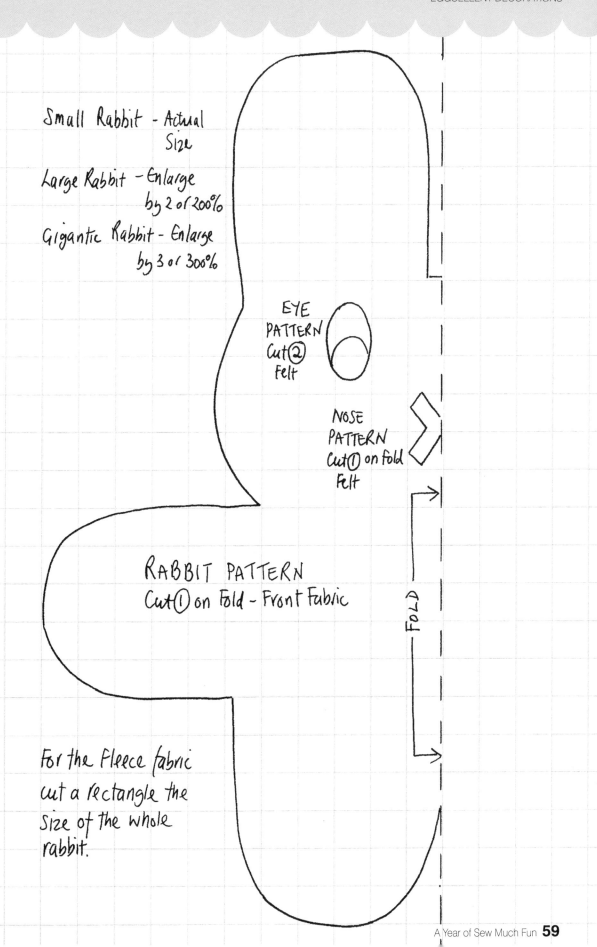

Small Rabbit - Actual Size

Large Rabbit - Enlarge by 2 or 200%

Gigantic Rabbit - Enlarge by 3 or 300%

EYE PATTERN
Cut② Felt

NOSE PATTERN
Cut① on fold Felt

RABBIT PATTERN
Cut① on Fold - Front Fabric

FOLD

For the Fleece fabric cut a rectangle the size of the whole rabbit.

MAGICAL MAY

Welcome new life

**THE MATERIALS
YOU WILL NEED:**

● 0.50 m for the first
patchwork fabric plus tie
● 1 fat quarter for the
second patchwork fabric
● 1 fat quarter for the th
patchwork fabric
● 0.60 m fleece
● 0.60 m wadding at
120 cm wide
● Matching thread
● Safety pins

Baby Mat

Many of my beginner students are mums-to-be, friends of new mums, aunties or grannies and this baby mat re-visits your patchwork skills and gets you used to sewing something a little larger.

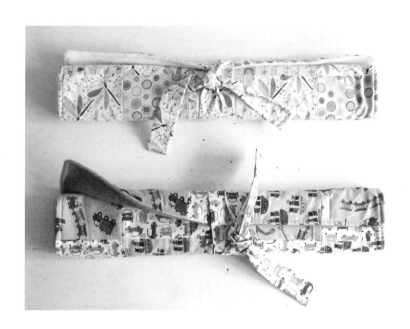

CUTTING INSTRUCTIONS
HOW TO MAKE IT

1 Cut 10 x 5" squares out of each patchwork fabric. Also cut two ties which measure 50 cm x 10 cm out of the first patchwork fabric. It is best to use a rotary knife and mat to cut out the squares but if you don't have these tools its not a problem just cut out the squares very accurately.

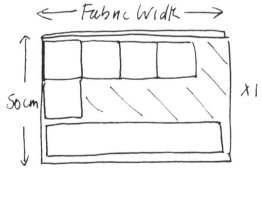

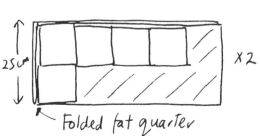

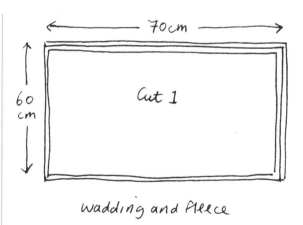

For the backing, cut out a piece of fleece 60 cm x 70 cm and for the middle, a piece of wadding the same size.

2 You need to sew five rows of six squares so first decide how to order the squares. The illustrations show a diagonal pattern but you can be as random as you like. Then, sewing your right sides together, join your squares in strips using a foot width seam allowance. Press the seams open.

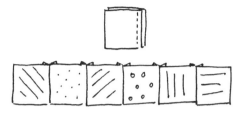

3 Taking your five strips, sew them right sides together again with a foot width seam allowance. Press the seams open.

4 To make the ties, fold in half lengthwise with right sides together. Then sew using a 1 cm seam allowance across one end and along the long side leaving the end open for turning through. Turn through and press flat.

5 Attach the ties at the middle of the shorter side on the right side. Sew in place.

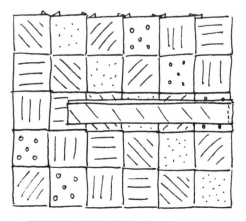

6 Taking all three layers (patchwork with ties attached, fleece and wadding), line them up on top of each other with the right side of the patchwork and fleece facing one another and then the wadding behind the fleece. Make sure the ties are lying flat down the middle so they do not get caught with the stitching.

Smoothing out all layers from the centre, safety pin together from the middle outwards. Pin around the edge then sew around using a 1 cm seam allowance and leaving a gap to turn through.

7 Unpin and turn through then lay out flat. To help keep it flat at the edges and sew up the gap, sew a top stitch row through all layers all the way around the mat.

ROZ'S TIP

Patchwork is about cutting and sewing accurately. But please do not worry if your squares are not perfect – just enjoy yourself!

5" square

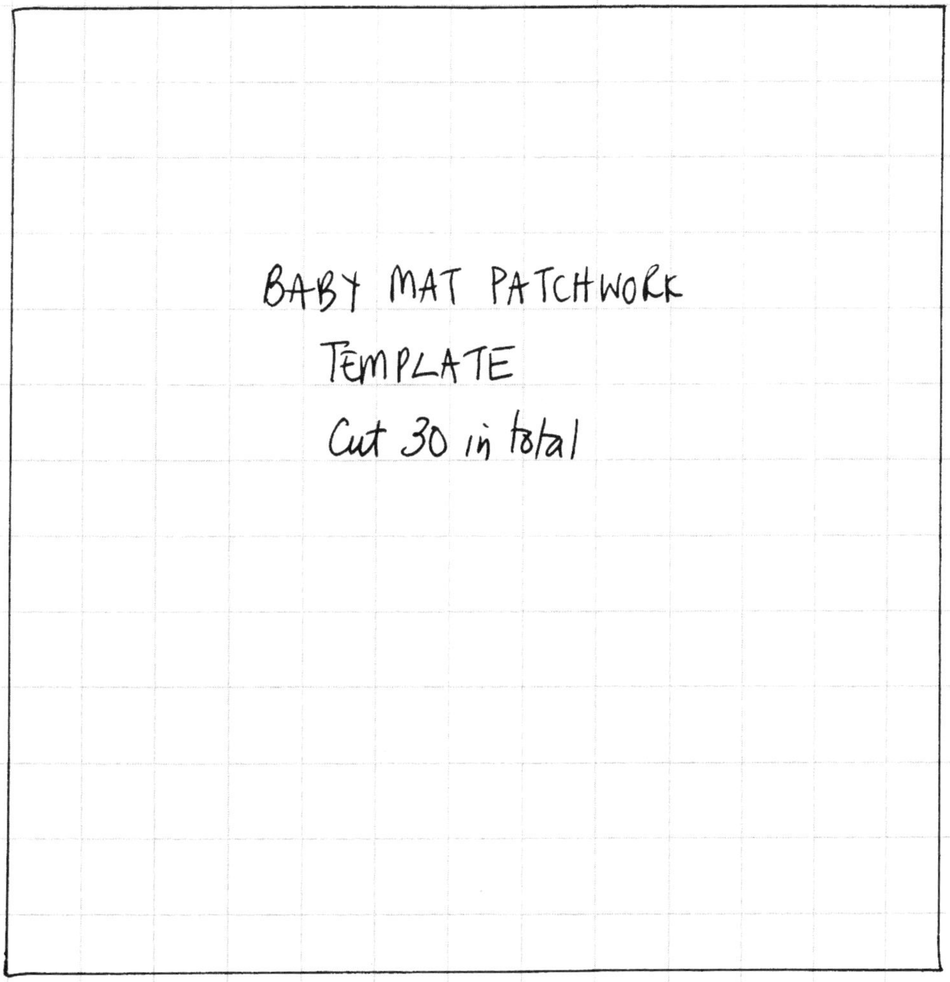

BABY MAT PATCHWORK
TEMPLATE
Cut 30 in total

THE MATERIALS YOU WILL NEED:

- 0.60 m fabric for angel dress (for the largest size)
- 1 m of 5 mm elastic
- 0.25 m for hand made binding or 0.65 m of ready-made bias binding
- Matching thread
- Safety pin

Baby Outfits
Angel Dress

These outfits for infants make great gifts and will introduce you to making clothes with sewn channels for elastic. The appliquéd baby grow shows you the technique for personalising ready-made items.

CUTTING INSTRUCTIONS
HOW TO MAKE IT

1 Enlarge the pattern by two on the fold. With the wrong sides together cut out a front and back.

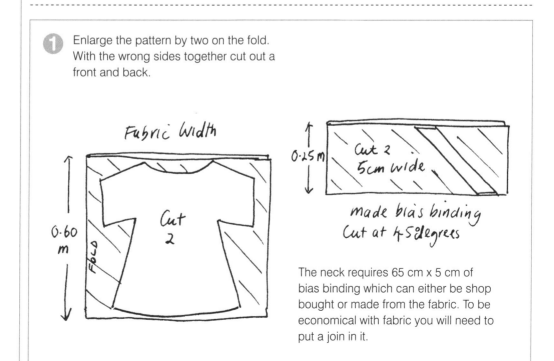

Fabric Width

0.60 m

FOLD

Cut 2

0.25 m

Cut 2 5cm wide

made bias binding Cut at 45 degrees

The neck requires 65 cm x 5 cm of bias binding which can either be shop bought or made from the fabric. To be economical with fabric you will need to put a join in it.

2 With a 1 cm seam allowance, sew the shoulder seams and side seams together. Snip in under the arms for a better fit then neaten all these seams with a zigzag stitch.

Snip corner

Sew 1cm seam on shoulder and side seams

3 Finish off the sleeves by using a 1 cm double-folded hem leaving a gap to thread in the elastic.

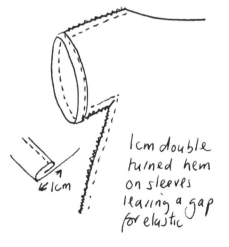

← 1cm

1cm double turned hem on sleeves leaving a gap for elastic

4 Finish off the hem by using a 1 cm double-folded hem.

and again at the hem no gap for elastic

5 Join the bias binding together at an angle and iron in half. Sew the binding around the neck by lining up all raw edges onto the right side of the dress, pin and sew with a 1 cm seam. At the beginning of your sewing, tuck in your binding end. Turn the binding over onto the wrong side of the fabric and sew along the folded edge creating a channel for the elastic. Leave a gap to thread in the elastic.

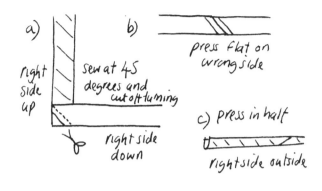

a)
right side up
sew at 45 degrees and cut off turning
right side down

b)
press flat on wrong side

c) press in half
right side outside

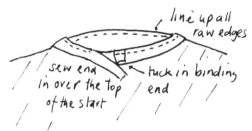

line up all raw edges
sew end in over the top of the start
tuck in binding end

Flip folded edge of binding to the wrongside and sew down at folded edge

gap for elastic

6 Using a safety pin, thread through the elastic into the neck and the two sleeves. With 5 mm of elastic it is easiest to knot the ends together. Then sew up all the gaps.

Elastic measurements

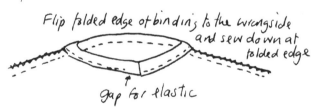

	6 months	1 year	18 months	2 years	
neck	50 cms	51 cms	52 cms	53 cms	x 1
arm holes	20 cms	21 cms	22 cms	23 cms	x 2

measurements include a 5cm allowance for tieing knots

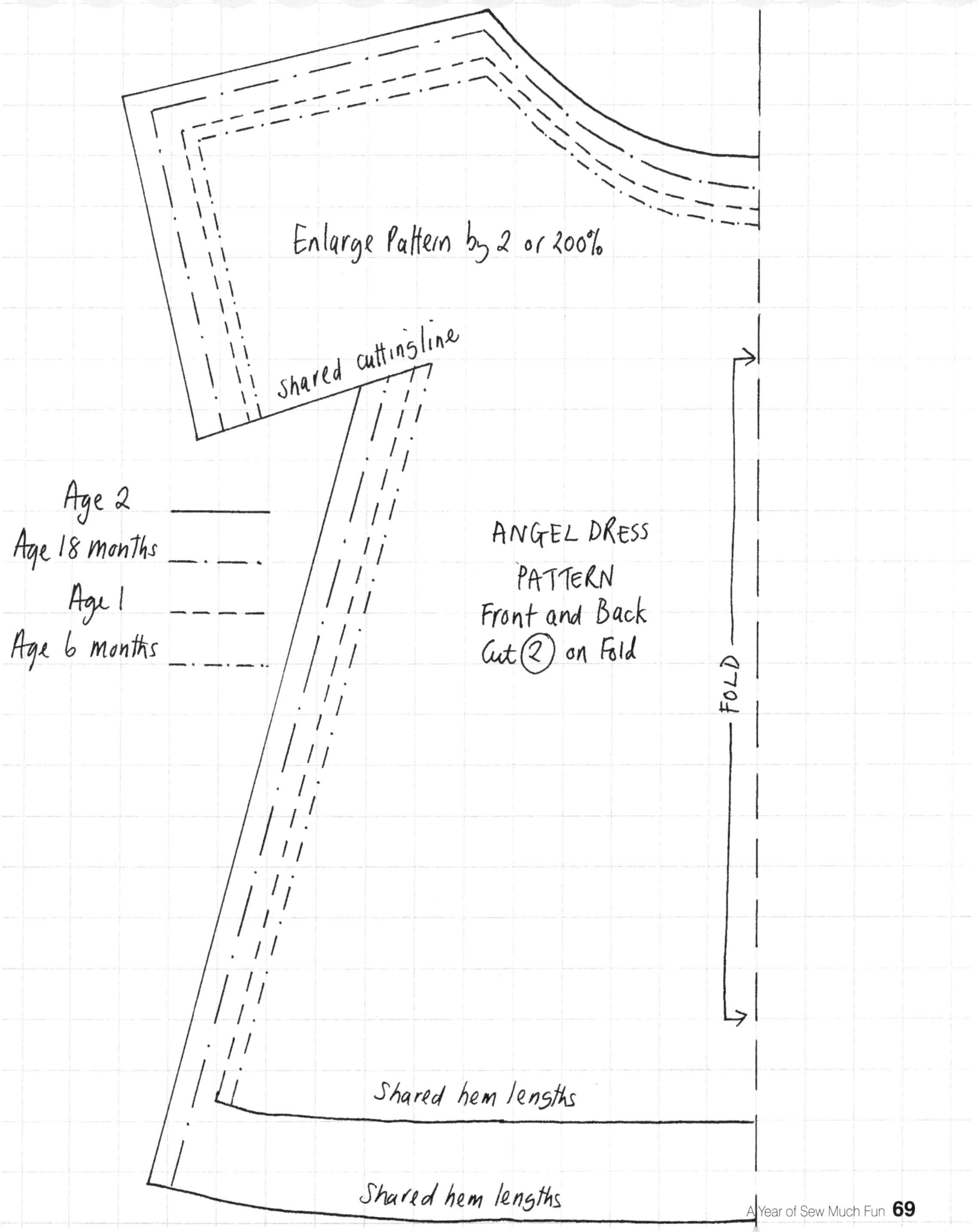

Enlarge Pattern by 2 or 200%

shared cuttingline

Age 2 _____

Age 18 months _·_·_·_

Age 1 _ _ _ _ _

Age 6 months _··_··_··_

ANGEL DRESS
PATTERN
Front and Back
Cut ② on Fold

FOLD

Shared hem lengths

Shared hem lengths

THE MATERIALS YOU WILL NEED:

- 0.40 m cotton bloomer fabric
- 0.50 m elastic 15 mm wide
- 0.80 m elastic 5 mm wide
- Matching thread
- Safety pin

THE MATERIALS YOU WILL NEED:

- 1 ready-made cotton baby grow
- 10 cms square of interlining
- Scraps of washable felt
- Matching thread and white for the eye

Baby Outfits – Bloomers, and Appliquéd Baby Grow

When threading elastic through a channel with a safety pin, always pin the other end to the fabric near the gap to make sure it doesn't follow you into the channel requiring you to start all over again.

If you have little time just buy a ready-made item and personalise it with felt appliqué.

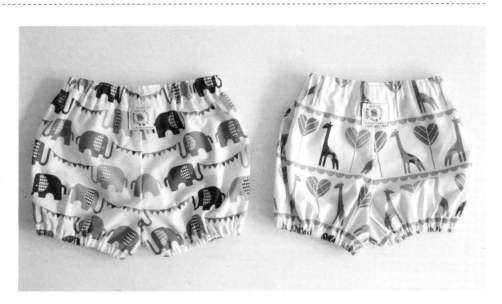

CUTTING INSTRUCTIONS
HOW TO MAKE IT

1 Enlarge the pattern by two. With wrong sides together cut out a pair of the bloomers.

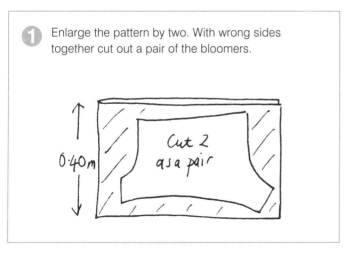

2 With right sides together sew the front and back rise seam using a 1 cm seam allowance. Neaten these seams with a zigzag stitch.

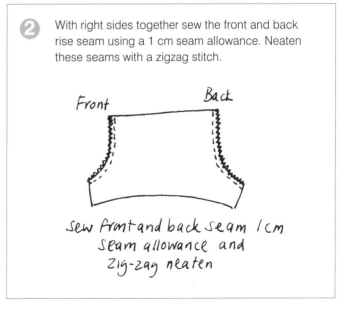

3 With right sides together place these two seams together at the crutch and sew the crutch seam. Neaten with a zigzag stitch.

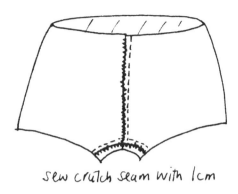

sew crutch seam with 1cm

4 Around the waist make a 3 cm double-folded hem to create a channel for the waist elastic. Pin and sew along the folded down edge and along the top edge.

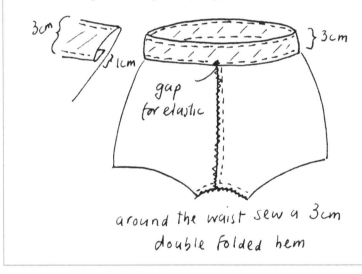

3cm
1cm
3cm
gap for elastic

around the waist sew a 3cm double folded hem

5 Finish off the leg hems by using a 1 cm double-folded hem leaving a gap to thread in the elastic.

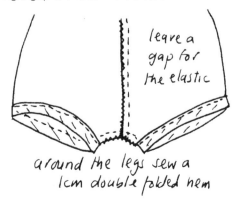

leave a gap for the elastic

around the legs sew a 1cm double folded hem

6 When the correct length has been achieved (see below), and you have made sure there is no twist in the elastic, cut off the excess and place one end of the elastic over the other end and sew together with a square of stitching.

Elastic Measurements

Cms	6 months	1 year	18 months	
Waist	46 cms	48 cms	50 cms	x 1
legs	25 cms	26 cms	27 cms	x 2

7 Using a safety pin, thread the 5 mm elastic through the leg hems until the required length has been achieved. With a 5 mm elastic it is easiest to knot the ends together. Then sew up all the gaps.

Thread elastic through channels using safety pin

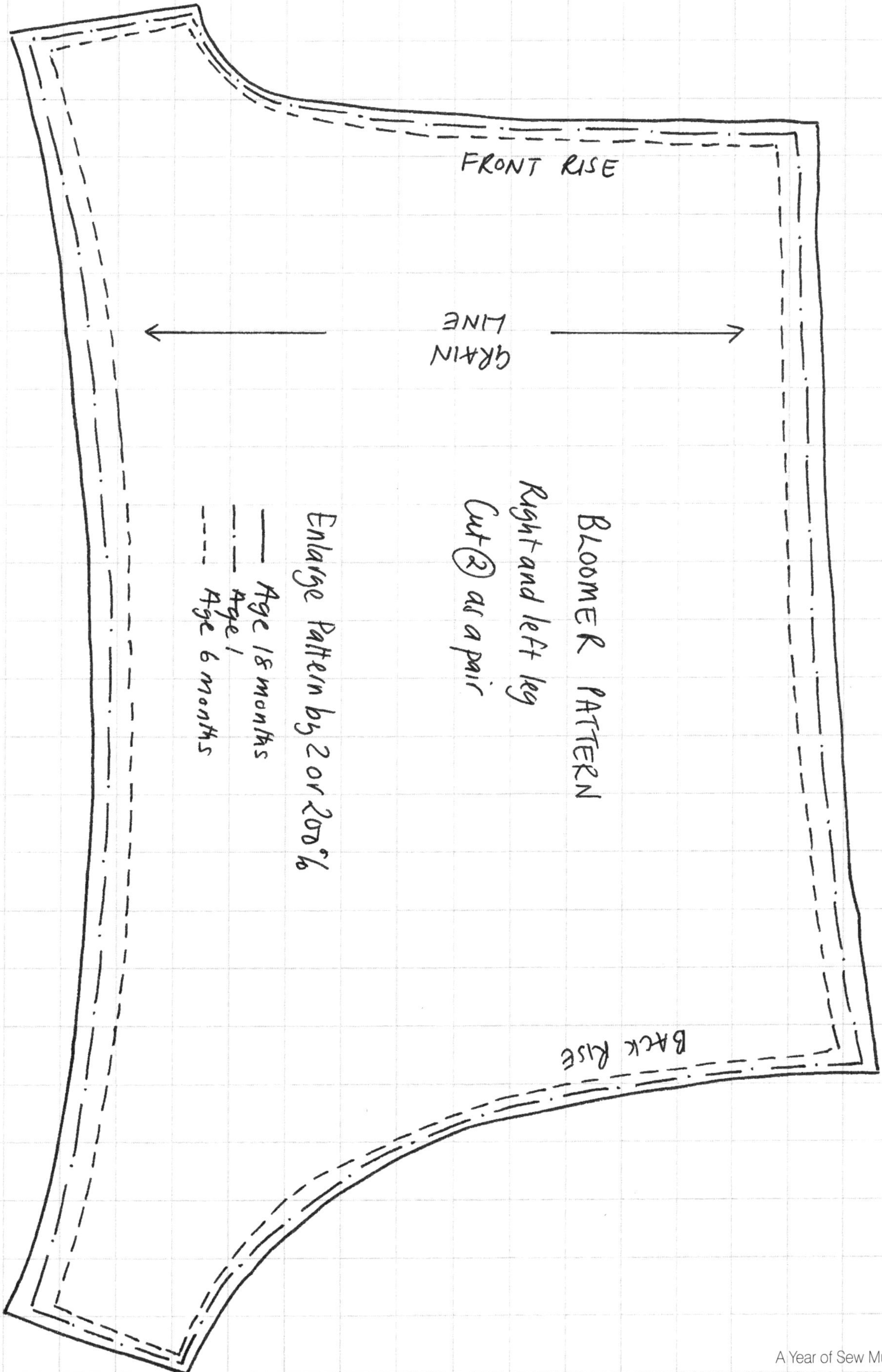

FRONT RISE

GRAIN LINE

BLOOMER PATTERN

Right and left leg

Cut ② as a pair

Enlarge pattern by 2 or 200%

——— Age 18 months

—·—· Age 1

- - - Age 6 months

Back Rise

1 Copy out the giraffe pattern and cut it out of felt.

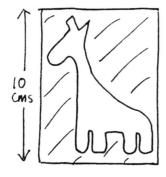

10 CMS

2 Turn the baby grow inside out and iron on a square of interlining that will be big enough for your appliqué design.

3 Sew on the eye of the giraffe using a satin stitch. Then pin on the giraffe shape in the middle of the front of the baby grow, above the waist and sew on using a running stitch. Then sew on the patches. Make sure all your stitching is securely cast on and off.

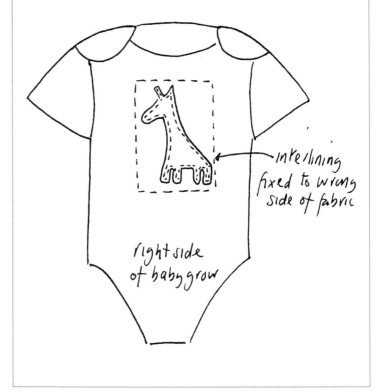

interlining fixed to wrong side of fabric

right side of babygrow

ROZ'S TIP

You can use this process with any design but please do not add any buttons or trinkets that could end up being a choking hazard for the baby.

Actual Pattern Size

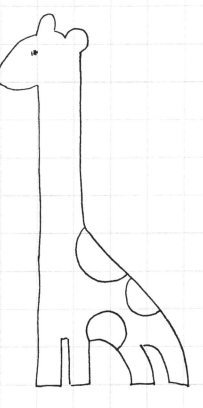

N.B. This is not one of my designs we just
copied it from the fabric we made the bloomers in so
they matched.

JAZZY JUNE

A perfect day for a picnic

THE MATERIALS YOU WILL NEED:
To make two cushions

- 0.6 m of cushion fabric
- 0.6 m of waterproof fabric
- 50 cm square ready-made cushion pad
- 2.20 m co-ordinating 15mm bias tape
- 2.20 m of piping cord
- 45 cm zip
- Zipper foot
- Thread that matches the bias tape
- Thread that matches the waterproof lining

Picnic Cushion

Picnic in style with this cosy cushion. This project introduces you to the technique of bias binding and piping. The cushion also features a zip and waterproof bottom to protect it from the great British weather.

CUTTING INSTRUCTIONS
HOW TO MAKE IT

1 Cut out a 52 cm square of the top fabric. Cut out a 52 cm x 56 cm rectangle of the waterproof lining and then cut the lining in two – creating a 52 cm x 48 cm piece and a 52 cm x 8 cm piece. These pieces will be used for the zip opening.

← Fabric Width →

0·6 m

Cut 1
52 cm
square

0·6m

Cut 1
52cm x 48cm

52cm x 8cm

2 To make piping you need a length of ready-made bias binding, piping cord and a zipper foot. Open up your bias binding and wrap it around your cord with the right side on the outside so your raw edges meet. Then, using your zipper foot, stitch as closely to the cord as you can. You can pin all 2.2 m in place first and then sew, or you can just manage trapping the cord into the binding with your fingers in lots of short stages at the machine.

ready made bias binding

zipper foot

cord

wrap the binding around the cord and sew close to the cord with a zipper foot

You need to make 2·20 m worth

3 Taking your cushion fabric, place your ready-made piping around the edge of the square making sure the rolled edge is facing towards the centre of the cushion and all raw edges are lined up around the outside edge. To get smooth and even corners make three snips in the piping to enable you to bend the piping around the corner. Pin and sew in place following the stitch line you have already made on the piping, leaving a gap and an overlap of piping to make a neat join.

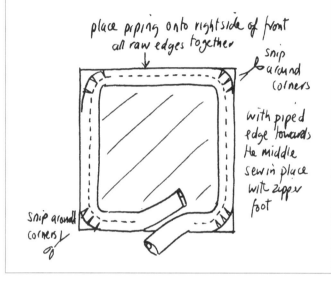

place piping onto rightside of front
all raw edges together

snip around corners

with piped edge towards the middle sew in place with zipper foot

snip around corners

4 To make a neat join first cut the two piping cords so they butt up to each other, be careful not to cut the binding. Take one side of the bias binding and fold in 1 cm and then with the other side of the binding trim and tuck into the binding with the fold. Sew all of this in place.

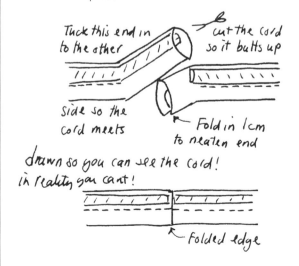

Tuck this end in to the other

cut the cord so it butts up

Side so the cord meets

Fold in 1cm to neaten end

drawn so you can see the cord! in reality you can't!

Folded edge

5 With the two back pieces create a 1 cm single fold on the small side and a 2 cm fold on the large side. Use your fingernails to create these folds as the iron has a tendency to melt waterproof lining.

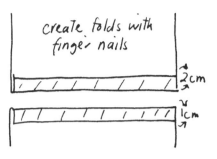

create folds with finger nails

2cm

1cm

6 Place the zip under the 1 cm fold and sew in place using the zipper foot close to the edge of the fold. Place the 2 cm folded edge over the zip so it is covered and sew in place.

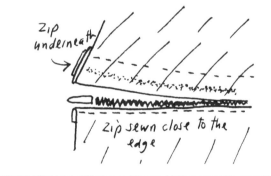

zip underneath

zip sewn close to the edge

ROZ'S TIP

If you are using a feather-filled cushion pad, cut the cushion pattern slightly smaller to ensure you get a puffy cushion.

With right sides of the cushion together, unzip the zipper half way down and pin all around the cushion on the side with a stitch line to follow. Sew all around the cushion with the zipper foot following this seam line. Trim turnings and zigzag together to neaten the seams. Then turn the cushion through the zipper opening. Fill it with your cushion pad.

on other side undo zip place right sides together

sew seam all the way around following existing stitch line with the zipper foot

THE MATERIALS YOU WILL NEED:
To make two cushions

● 1.20 m of bag fabric and lining fabric
(you could choose a different lining fabric but
that would mean you only need 0.6 m of each)
● 0.50 m wadding at 120 cm wide
● 6 x 30 cm of co-ordinating felt squares
● 1.50 m of colourful 35 mm wide webbing
● Thread that matches the bag fabric
● Thread that matches the felt
● Thread that matches the webbing

Beach Bag

This holiday essential is big enough to fit everything you need for a day out and looks lovely too.

This project introduces you to wadding and the concept of lining and 'bagging out'.

CUTTING INSTRUCTIONS
HOW TO MAKE IT

1 Cut out a rectangular pattern 55 cm x 45 cm. Using this pattern cut out two outer fabrics, two lining fabrics and two pieces of wadding. Using the beach hut pattern cut out three beach huts, three roofs, three doors, one lot of vertical 1 cm stripes, one lot of horizontal 2 cm stripes, a heart and eight bunting flags.

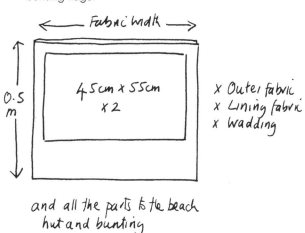

2 So you do not keep on having to change your sewing threads on the machine all the time create one hut at a time and sew it on the bag 7 cm up from the bottom with a central position. Sew the stripes, doors and heart on first and then the hut onto the front panel of the bag and the roof on at the end. At the centre the bunting is 13 cm down from the top and at the sides 6 cm down from the top.

edge stitch beach hut decoration

Edge stitch huts onto front of bag, then roof, then bunting

If you do not want to fiddle around with lots of thread colours just use a colour that matches the background.

3 Taking your front and back panel of the bag, sew on the wadding to the wrong side all the way around the edge with a seam allowance that is smaller than 1 cm. Then with the rights sides together sew around three edges (not along the opening) on the bag with a 1 cm seam allowance.

attach wadding to wrong side of outer fabric ×2

← Outer fabric

right sides together sew 1cm seam through all thicknesses

4 Taking your lining panels right sides together sew 1 cm around the same three seams but leaving a gap in the seam along the bottom.

lining right side together sew 1cm seam

← gap →

5 A mock gusset helps create some depth to the bag. With the bag still right sides together line up the side seam and bottom two seams to make a point. Sew across 5 cm from the point from edge to edge. Repeat this on the corner of the bag and the two corners of the lining.

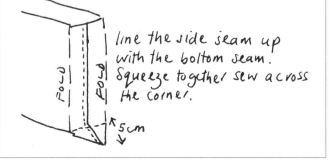

line the side seam up with the bottom seam. Squeeze together sew across the corner.

5cm

6 Turn the bag lining so it has the right side on the outside and place in the outer bag which you have not turned through. With the right sides together line up the top raw edges, matching the sides seam and sew all around the top with a 1 cm seam.

with right sides together drop lining inside the bag

sew around the top with a 1cm seam

7 Using the gap created in step 4, pull the whole bag through, sew up the gap with an edge stitch and stuff the lining into the bag. To keep in place, topstitch through all the layers around the top. Cutting the webbing into two lengths of 75 cm, fold under the end and sew in place on the outside of the bag 15 cm in and 4 cm down. Sew on with a square of secure sewing.

ROZ'S TIP

A mock gusset is a simple way to add depth to a bag.

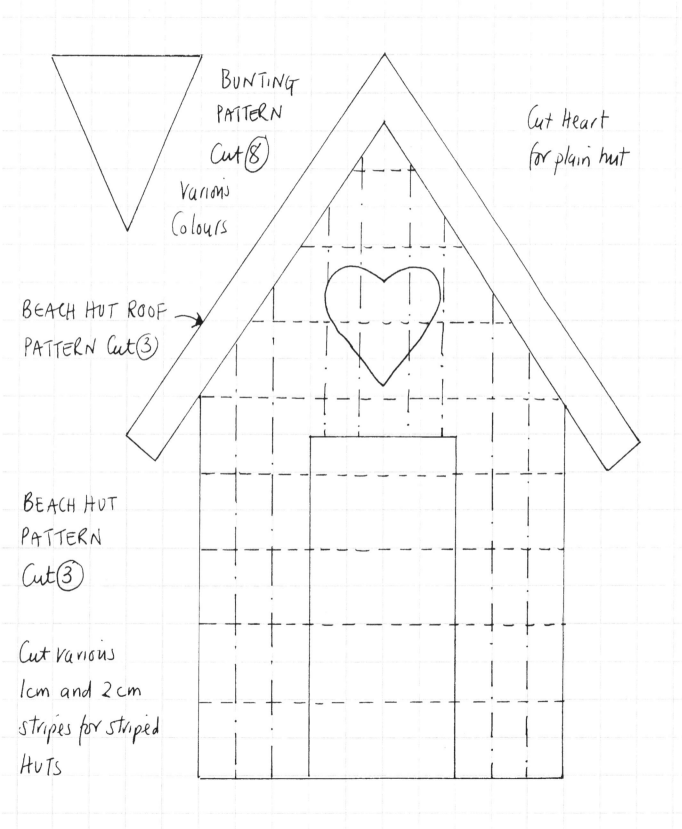

BUNTING PATTERN
Cut (8)
Various Colours

Cut Heart for plain hut

BEACH HUT ROOF PATTERN Cut (3)

BEACH HUT PATTERN
Cut (3)

Cut various 1cm and 2cm stripes for striped HUTS

JUBILANT JULY

We're all going on a summer holiday!

THE MATERIALS YOU WILL NEED:

Wash bag
- 0.30 m bag fabric
- 0.30 m of waterproof fabric
- 25 cm zip
- Thread which matches the bag fabric
- Thread which matches the lining fabric

Make-up bag
- 0.30 m bag fabric
- 0.30 m of waterproof fabric
- 18 cm zip
- Thread which matches the bag fabric
- Thread which matches the lining fabric

Both of these bags are made in the same way the only difference is that the zips and bags are different sizes.

Wash and Make-up Bag

Find yourself reviewing the state of your wash bag every time you go away? Then why not make your own. Another favourite at Sew Much Fun, this project allows you to tackle zips in a non-threatening way.

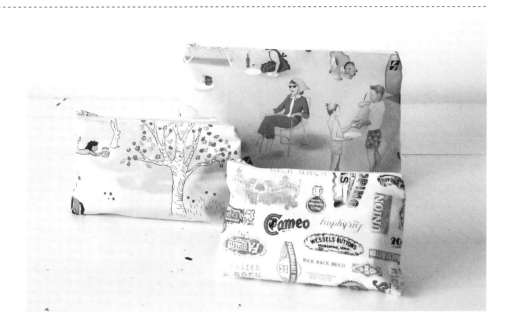

CUTTING INSTRUCTIONS
HOW TO MAKE IT

1 Copy the wash bag pattern on the fold and use this pattern to cut two out of the bag fabric and two out of the waterproof lining fabric. Make sure you realise the top of the bag is the side without the squares cut out so if you have a one-way fabric make sure the pattern is running in the right direction.

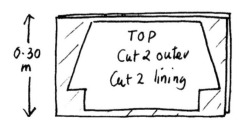

2 To prepare for the zip insertion you need to fold over a 1 cm seam towards the wrong side of the wash bag fabric. Press in place. Repeat again for the lining but do not press just use your finger nails to make a crease. It is very easy to melt the waterproof lining with the iron.

3 Pin your creased lining onto the wrong side of your zip keeping the right side of your lining uppermost (so you don't see your turning). Using your zipper foot sew on the zip evenly.

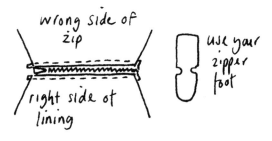

4 Turning your zip over to the right side, pin on your pressed wash bag fabric, each side of the zip with the right side of the fabric uppermost. Sew your zip on again using your zipper foot.

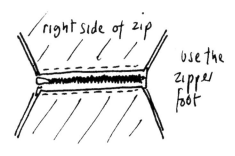

5 Unzip the zipper half way down and place your right sides of the bag together. Line up evenly, trim if necessary using the existing angles as a guide and pin together.

6 Sew the seams with a 1 cm seam allowance but do not sew the cut out squares. Neaten these three seams with a zigzag stitch.

7 Open up the cut out corners and fold together diagonally matching the seams together. Sew across this diagonal with a 1 cm seam allowance. Trim and neaten with a zigzag stitch.

ROZ'S TIP

There are many ways of sewing in zips but these are great projects to help you become more confident with your zip insertion. Always remember practice makes perfect!

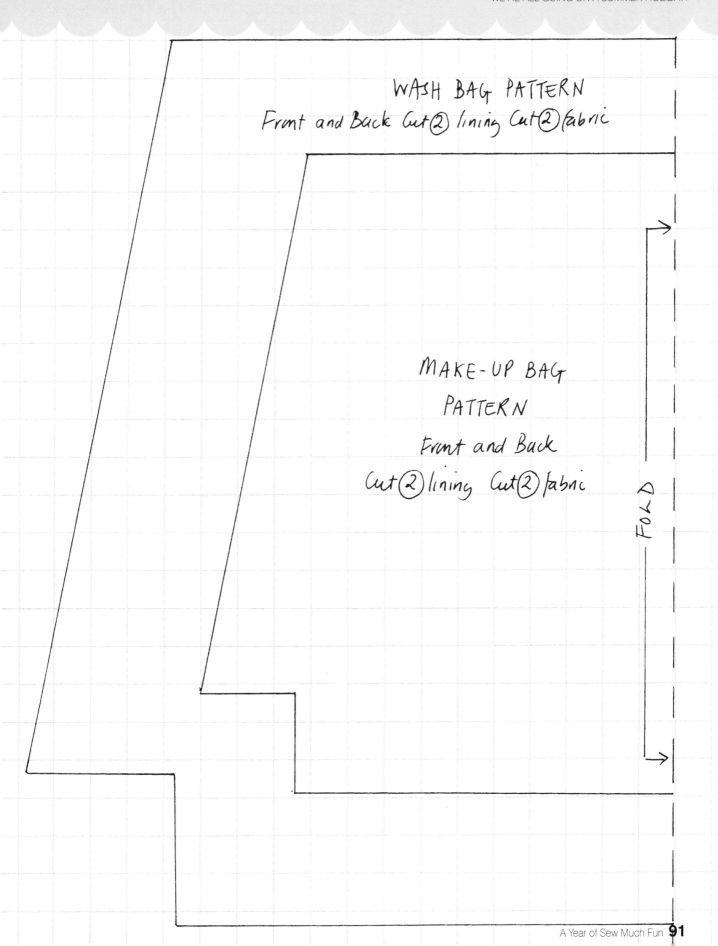

WASH BAG PATTERN
Front and Back Cut ② lining Cut ② fabric

MAKE-UP BAG
PATTERN
Front and Back
Cut ② lining   Cut ② fabric

FOLD

THE MATERIALS
YOU WILL NEED:

- 0.80 m of PJ shorts fabric, 110 cms wide or,
- 0.40 m of PJ shorts fabric, 150 ms wide
- 1 m of 20 mm wide elastic
- 0.20 m of decorative trim for pocket
- Thread which matches the PJ short fabric
- 1 safety pin

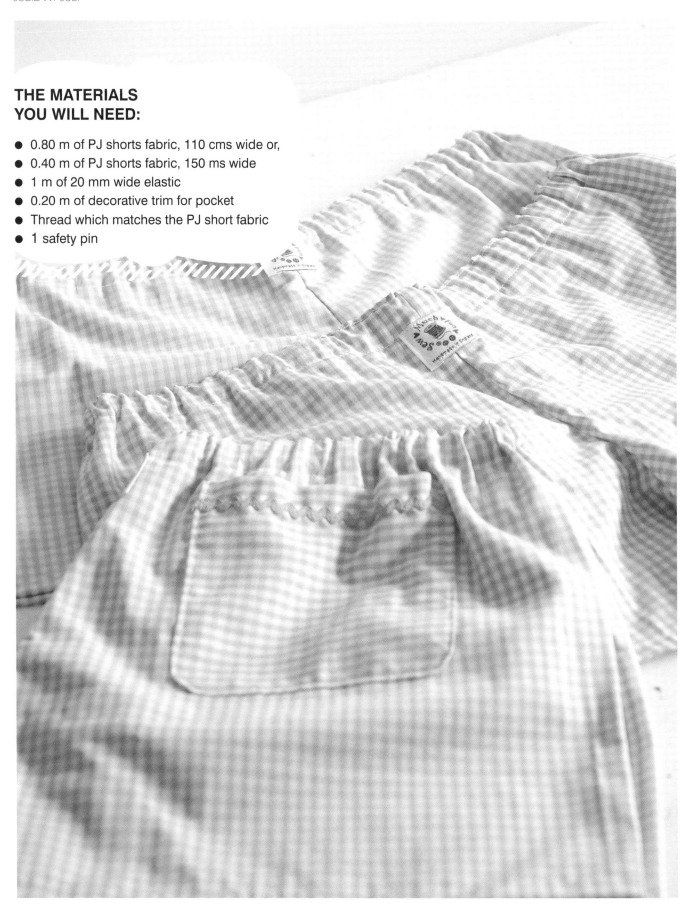

Boxy PJ Shorts

Ideal for wandering around the house and sleeping in the heat, these unisex shorts see you making something for yourself or your growing children.

CUTTING INSTRUCTIONS
HOW TO MAKE IT

1. Enlarge the pyjama shorts pattern and pocket by three. Then cut out a pair of the shorts pattern and one pocket on the fold.

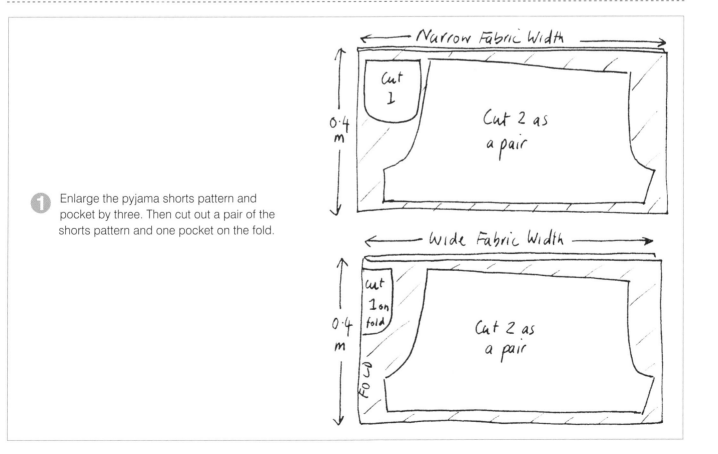

2 Take the pocket and make a 1 cm double-turned hem along the straight edge. On the right side of the pocket, sew on the trim over the top of the row of the double-turned stitch line. Sew around the rest of the pocket with a 1 cm seam allowance. Snip the corners and using the line of sewing press the turning towards the wrong side ready for sewing onto the PJ shorts.

press towards the back

snip

3 Take the right side of the shorts and sew on the pocket 8 cm in from the back rise and approximately 7 cm down from the top.

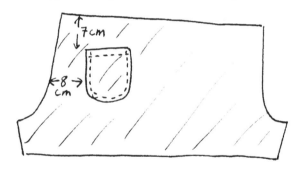

7cm

8 cm

4 Placing the right sides of the shorts together sew the front and back rise seams with a 1 cm seam allowance. Neaten with a zigzag stitch. Place these two seams together at the crutch and sew together with a 1 cm seam allowance. Neaten with a zigzag stitch.

Sew 1cm seam on the front and back rise.

5 Around the waist make a 3 cm double-folded hem to make a channel for the waist elastic. Pin and sew along the folded down edge leaving a gap for the elastic. Then sew all around the top edge. Hem up the short legs with a 1 cm double-folded hem.

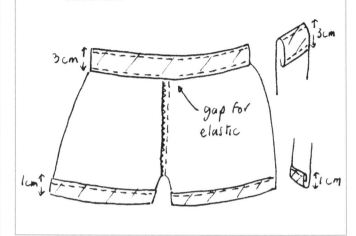

3cm

3cm

gap for elastic

1cm

1 cm

6 Measure off the required elastic (if you are making them to fit), or use the measurement chart below. Using a safety pin, thread the 20 mm elastic through the waistband. Making sure there is no twist in the elastic, place one end of elastic over the other end and sew together with a square of stitching. Sew up the gap.

Either measure your own hip measurement or below as a guide

	Size 6	Size 8	Size 10
Waist/hip	70 cm	75 cm	80 cm

ROZ'S TIP

To make PJ bottoms, just add extra length to the legs using your inside leg measurement as a guide.

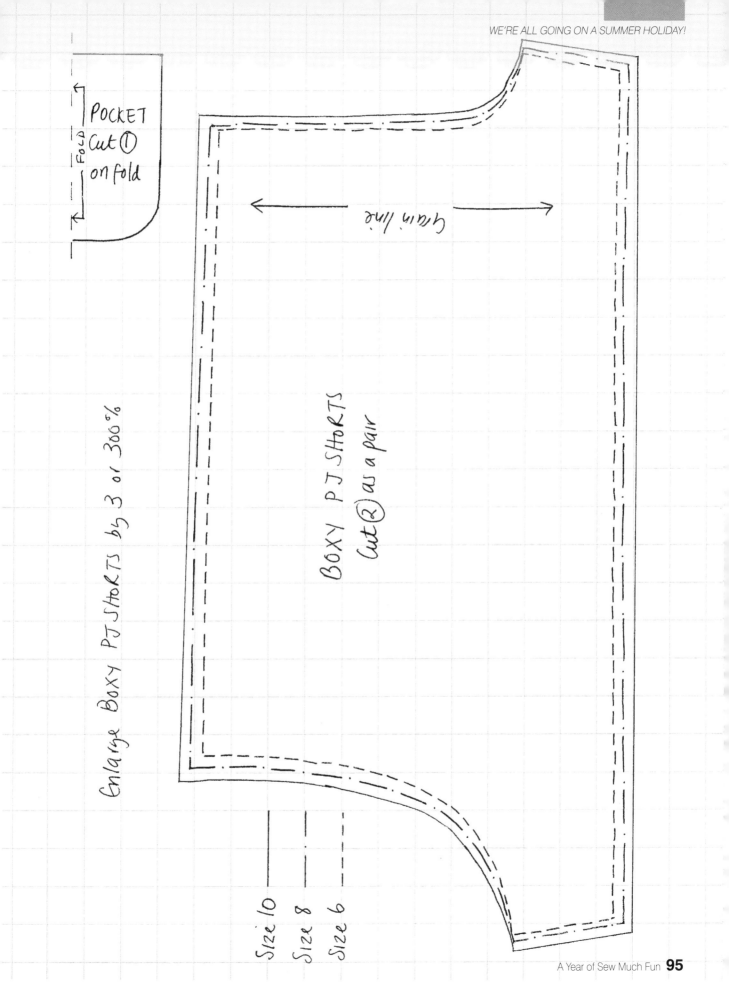

POCKET
Cut ①
on fold

FOLD

Grain line

BOXY PJ SHORTS
Cut ② as a pair

Enlarge BOXY PJ SHORTS by 3 or 300%

Size 10 ——————
Size 8 —·—·—·—·—
Size 6 — — — — —

ACTIVE AUGUST

Going out and about

THE MATERIALS YOU WILL NEED:

- 0.80 m of knitted towelling fabric, 150 cms wide
- 0.40 m of knitted lining fabric
- 0.30 m of cotton tape
- Thread which matches towelling fabric

Kids Hooded Top

This hooded top made from knitted towelling is not as complicated as it looks and with guidance you will be really pleased with the result. This also makes a great beach cover-up to protect kids from the sun.

CUTTING INSTRUCTIONS
HOW TO MAKE IT

1 Enlarge all the hooded top patterns by three. Cut out one front and back on the fold, one pocket on the fold, a pair of hoods and a pair of sleeves out of the knitted towelling fabric.

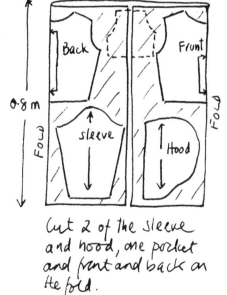

Cut 2 of the sleeve and hood, one pocket and front and back on the fold.

Using the same hood pattern cut out a pair from the lining fabric along with the pocket trim.

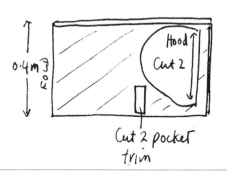

Cut 2 pocket trim

When sewing jersey on a domestic sewing machine, it is advisable to use a stitch with a bit of zigzag in it to give the seam a little extra thread to accommodate the stretch. Set your zigzag stitch to 1 mm in the stitch width and 3 mm in the stitch length to give you a shallow zigzag stitch.

shallow zig-zag

A jersey fabric tends not to fray so you do not need to zigzag the seams unless you just want the seams to look neater on the inside of your garment.

2 As with all sewing you need to decorate first so in this case we need to prepare the pocket. Fold the pocket trim in half lengthwise. At the diagonal of the pocket, sew the trim onto the right side of the pocket, lining up all raw edges. Then flip the trim over to the wrong side of the fabric leaving a little bit of the trim on show and then sew down the trim along the fold.

roll trim over to the back sew down

3 Press a 1 cm single fold hem around the rest of the pocket and place centrally onto the front pattern 21 cm (for size 5/6) 24 cm (for size 7/8) up from the hem. Sew in place making sure you secure your stitching carefully at the top and bottom of the pocket openings.

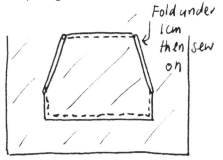

Fold under 1cm then sew on

4 To ensure the shoulder seams do not stretch out of shape or come undone due to excessive stretching, sew in a piece of cotton tape whilst sewing the shoulder seams. With right sides together and a strip of cotton tape, sew a 1 cm seam allowance to join your shoulder seams together.

Sew shoulder seams with a strip of cotton tape 1cm seam

5 With this loose fitting style you can attach the sleeves on the flat. With right sides together, line up the centre of your armhole with your shoulder seam. Keeping all raw edges lined up, pin the sleeve in place making sure you have matched up your front and back sleeve. Then sew the seams with a 1 cm seam allowance.

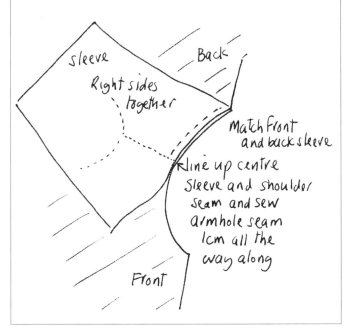

sleeve
Back
Right sides together
Match front and back sleeve
Line up centre sleeve and shoulder seam and sew armhole seam 1cm all the way along
Front

6 With your right sides together, line up your underarm seams and pin your arm and side seams together. Sew with a 1 cm seam allowance.

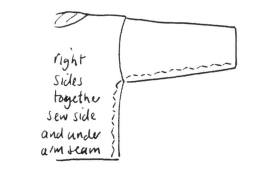

right sides together sew side and under arm seam

ROZ'S TIP

Stretchy fabrics are difficult to use but you can normally get away with more mistakes!

7 To make the hood: first sew the seam down the centre back with right sides together and a 1 cm seam on both the outer and lining fabric. Then, with right sides together, sew the front edge of the hood together with a 1 cm seam allowance. Turn the hood right side out. Roll out a little bit of the lining fabric so it shows on the right side and top stitch around the front edge of the hood to hold this in place.

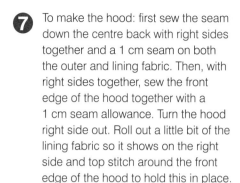

sew hood seam on outer and inner hood

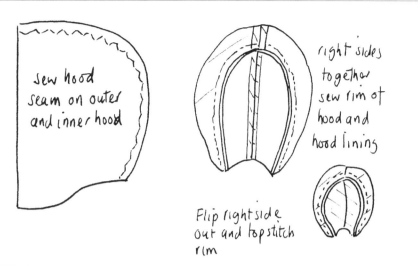

right sides together sew rim of hood and hood lining

Flip rightside out and topstitch rim

8 Treating the outer and inner fabric as one fabric, pin the hood to the neck line of the hooded top with right sides together. Line up the centre seam of the back of the hood to the centre back of the hooded top. Keeping all the raw edges in line, gentle ease the two curved shapes together bringing the two front edges together at the centre front of the hooded top. When you are happy with the positioning, sew together with a 1 cm seam allowance trying to avoid catching in any pleats. This is tricky so do not be worried if it takes you a couple of attempts – that is what your unpicker is for!

Once you have achieved this you need to trim away a little of the toweling fabric in the seam allowance. Then, sew down the lining seam to cover up all the unsightly turnings.

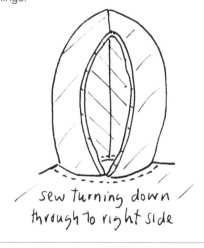

sew turning down through to right side

Trim away inside seam

right sides together line up bottom edge of hood with neck and sew with a 1cm seam

9 With the difficult bit over, all you need to do is hem the sleeves and hem with a 2 cm single-folded hem. Stitch just in from the raw edge.

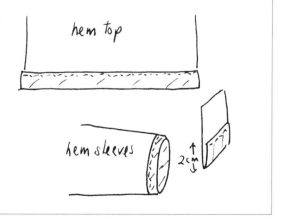

hem top

hem sleeves   2cm

Enlarge KIDS HOODED TOP by 3 or 300%

———————— Age 5-6
— · — · — · — Age 7-8

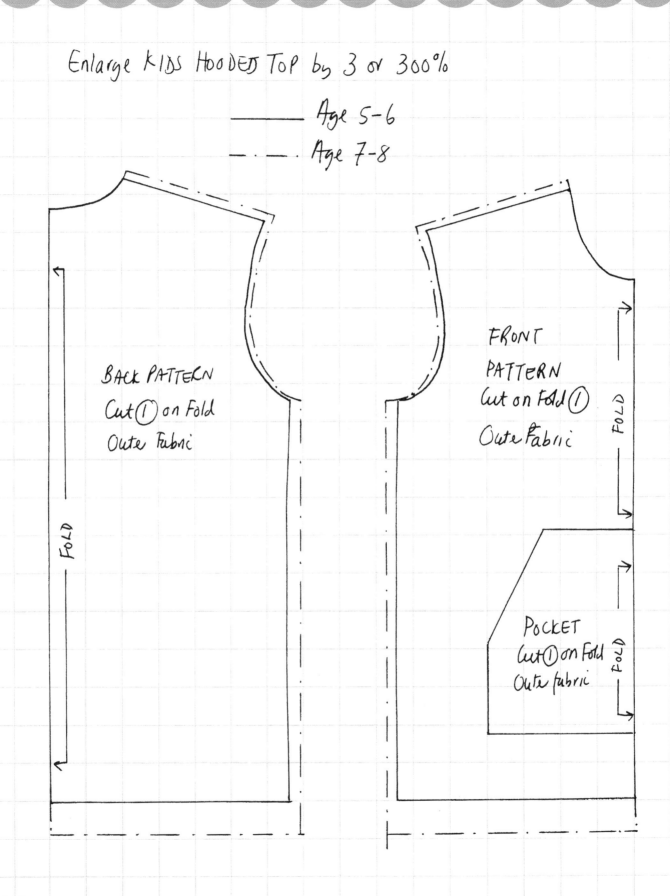

BACK PATTERN
Cut ① on Fold
Outer Fabric

FOLD

FRONT
PATTERN
Cut on Fold ①
Outer Fabric

FOLD

POCKET
Cut ① on Fold
Outer fabric

FOLD

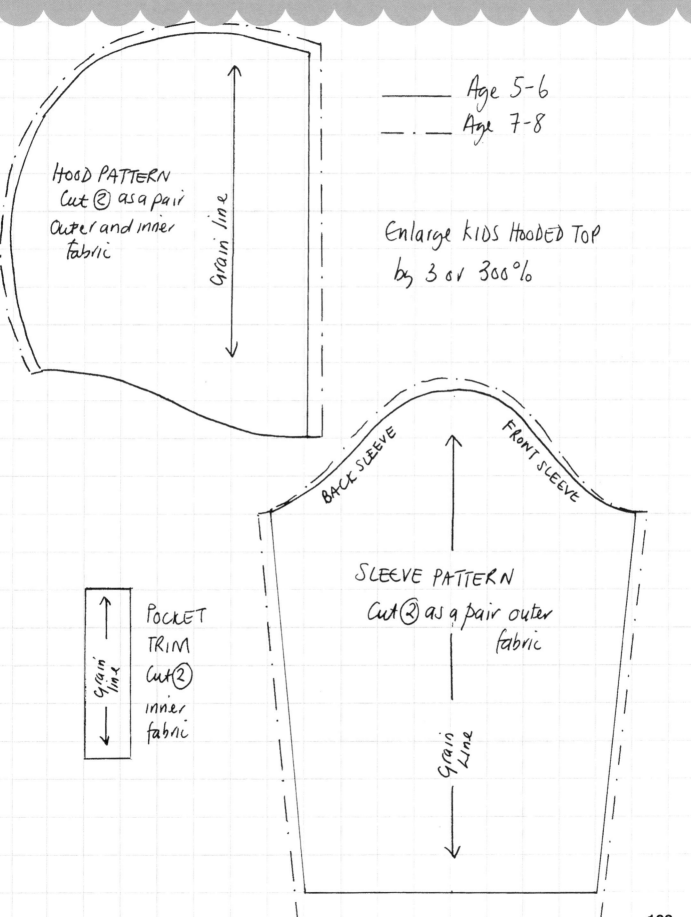

———— Age 5-6
—·—·— Age 7-8

HOOD PATTERN
Cut ② as a pair
Outer and inner fabric

Grain line

Enlarge KIDS HOODED TOP
by 3 or 300%

BACK SLEEVE

FRONT SLEEVE

SLEEVE PATTERN
Cut ② as a pair outer fabric

Grain line

POCKET TRIM
Cut ②
inner fabric

Grain line

THE MATERIALS YOU WILL NEED:
A skirt
- 0.50 m knitted skirt fabric, 150 cms wide
- 1 m of 20 mm wide elastic
- Matching thread

Shorts
- 0.50 m knitted short fabric, 150 cms wide
- 1 m of 20 mm wide elastic
- Matching thread

Kids Skirt and Shorts

To compliment the hooded top, make a pair of shorts or a skirt to match. They are so simple and quick to create you will wonder why anyone buys them!

CUTTING INSTRUCTIONS
HOW TO MAKE IT

1 Cut a 1 m x 0.36 cm piece to make a skirt for age 5/6.
Cut a 1 m x 0.39 cm piece to make a skirt for age 7/8.

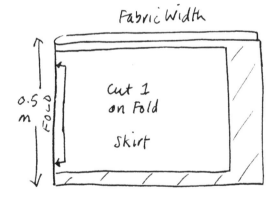

When sewing jersey on a domestic sewing machine, it is advisable to use a stitch with a bit of zigzag in it to give the seam a little extra thread to accommodate the stretch. Set your zigzag stitch to 1 mm in the stitch width and 3 mm in the stitch length to give you a shallow zigzag stitch.

Enlarge the shorts pattern by three and cut out a pair.

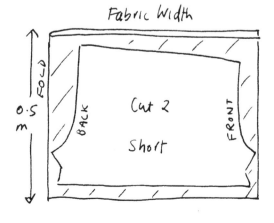

shallow zig-zag

1mm width

3mm length

3 SHORTS and SKIRT

Around the waist make a 4 cm single-folded hem to make a channel for the waist elastic. Pin and sew, stitching just in from the raw edge leaving a gap for the elastic. Then sew all around the top edge to create a nice finish to the top of the channel.

2 SHORTS

Placing the right sides of the shorts together, sew the front and back rise seams with a 1 cm seam allowance. Neaten seams with a zigzag stitch. Place these two seams together at the crutch seam and sew the crutch with a 1 cm seam allowance. Neaten the seam with a zigzag stitch.

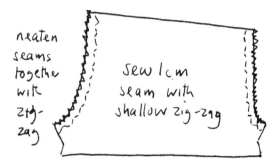

4

Hem up the short legs with a 2 cm single-folded hem. Hem up the skirt with a 2 cm single-folded hem.

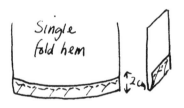

SKIRT

Placing the right sides together sew the back seam with a 1 cm seam allowance. Neaten the seam with a zigzag stitch.

5

Measure off the required elastic (if you are making them to fit), or use the measurement chart below. Using a safety pin, thread the 20 mm elastic through the waistband. Make sure there are no twists in the elastic. When you have done this, place one end of elastic over the other end and sew together with a square of stitching. Sew up the gap.

elastic measurements

	5/6	7/8
Waist	56-58 cms	59-60 cms

ROZ'S TIP

On an elastic channel always sew a row at the top as well as the bottom because it gives it a much nicer finish.

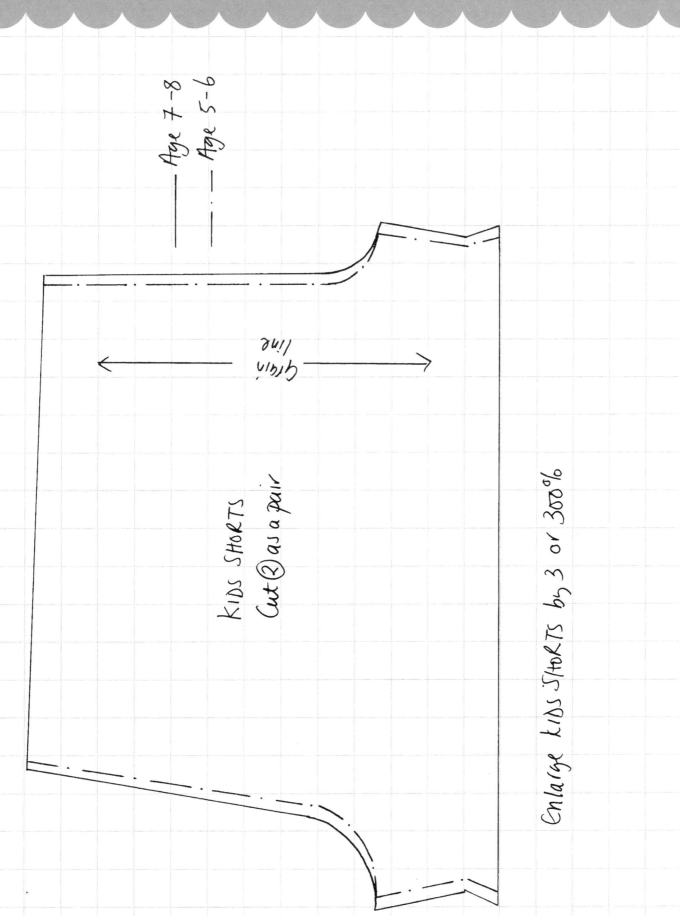

Age 7 - 8
Age 5 - 6

Grain line

KIDS SHORTS
Cut ② as a pair

Enlarge kids shorts by 3 or 300%

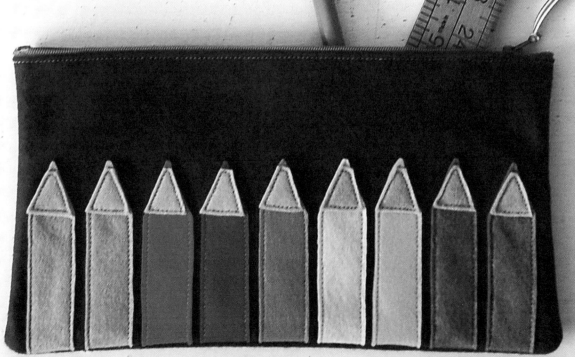

STUDIOUS SEPTEMBER

Getting ready for school

THE MATERIALS YOU WILL NEED:

- 1 x 30 cm square felt for the pencil case bag
- 1 x 15 cm square felt for the brown pencil
- 9 long thin felt scraps for the pencils
- 25 cm zip
- Thread to match the brown pencil
- 10 cm ribbon trim
- Zipper foot

Pencil Case

This essential item for every new school year can be unique and personalised if you make it yourself. We get all of our young sewing machine students to make pencil cases and the finished products are always so individual. They often result in orders from family and friends!

CUTTING INSTRUCTIONS
HOW TO MAKE IT

1 Cut the 30 cm square of felt in two. Copy out the pencil patterns and cut out of felt.

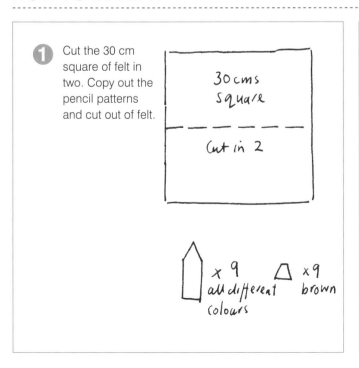

2 Take one side of the pencil case and place on the different coloured pencils, pin and sew on with an edge stitch. Make sure there is plenty of space around the pencils for the seam allowance on the pencil case. Then place on the brown pencil triangles showing a little bit of the colour at the top and sew them on with an edge stitch.

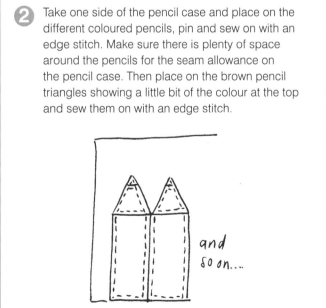

3 Attach the zip by pinning the top of the pencil case onto the zip. Using a zipper foot, sew it on with an edge stitch.

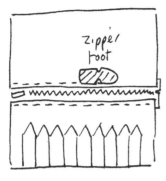

A straight edge stitch is always the neatest way to sew on felt.

4 Undo the zip half way and pin the pencil case with the right sides together. Sew around the outside of the pencil case making sure the stitch line sews over the zipper tape securely. Snip the excess fabric off at the corners and turn the pencil case through to the right side.

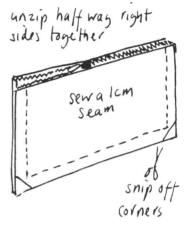

5 Tie on the ribbon to the end of the zipper tag.

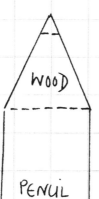

Actual size

PENCIL PATTERN
Cut ⑨ in a variety
of colours of felt
WOOD
Cut ⑨ in light brown felt

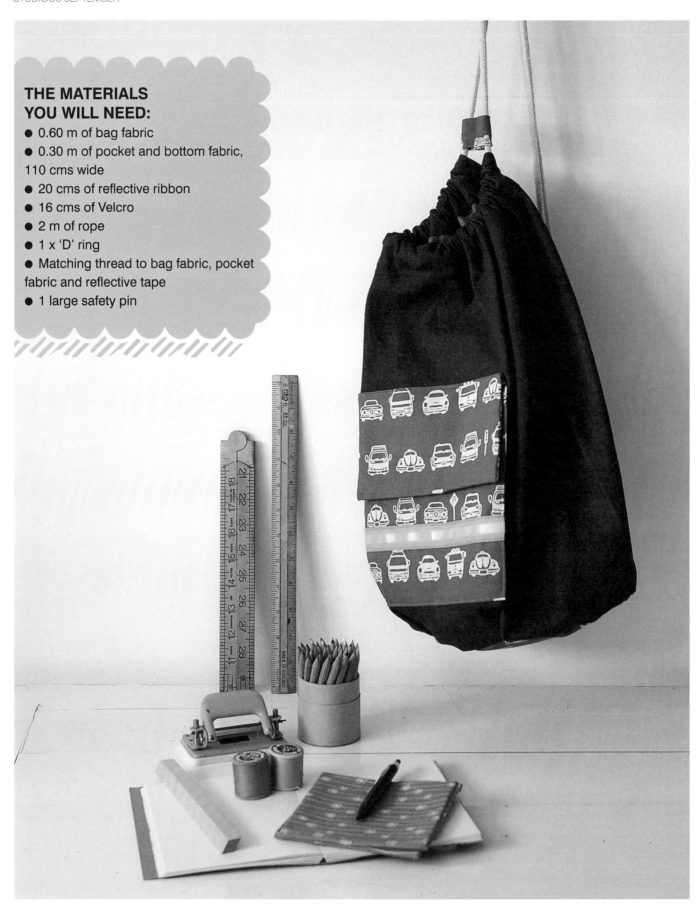

THE MATERIALS
YOU WILL NEED:

- 0.60 m of bag fabric
- 0.30 m of pocket and bottom fabric, 110 cms wide
- 20 cms of reflective ribbon
- 16 cms of Velcro
- 2 m of rope
- 1 x 'D' ring
- Matching thread to bag fabric, pocket fabric and reflective tape
- 1 large safety pin

Sports Duffle Bag

We always used duffle bags for our sports kit at school in the sixties, but this design has a more contemporary feel – adding reflective tape to allow kids to be seen in the dark. This project also introduces you to sewing on Velcro, a pocket with a flap, and sewing straight and curved edges together.

CUTTING INSTRUCTIONS
HOW TO MAKE IT

1 Cut out a rectangle 85 cm x 52 cm out of the bag fabric. Make a 15 mm snip 10 cm down on each of the 52 cm sides.

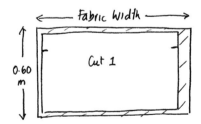

Enlarge the circle pattern by two on the fold and use this pattern to cut out two bottom fabrics. Cut out two rectangles 22 cms x 20 cms from the pocket fabric. One of these will be used to make the pocket flap. Copy out the tab and toggle pattern and cut out of the pocket fabric.

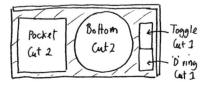

2 Before we make the pocket we have to attach the velcro and the reflective ribbon. At the top of one of the pocket pieces neaten with a 1 cm double-folded hem. Measure 7 cms down from this folded edge and sew on the soft side of the Velcro all the way around with an edge stitch. Then sew on the ribbon about 3 cm below it. Press a 1 cm seam allowance towards the wrong side of the pocket around the other three edges.

3 To make the pocket flap, fold the other pocket piece in two width wise and crease with the iron. Just below this crease sew on the hooked side of the Velcro all the way around. Then fold the crease the other way, placing the right sides together and sew the ends with a 1 cm seam allowance. Snip the corners and turn through and press flat. Neaten the raw edge with zigzag stitch and press a 1 cm seam allowance towards the wrong side of the flap.

4 Take the rectangle cut out in the bag fabric with the snips at the top and place the pocket in the middle, 24 cm down from the top. Pin in place and sew around three sides with an edge stitch. Then line up the pocket flap so the Velcro matches and sew on the top of the flap onto the bag with an edge stitch.

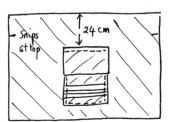

5 Taking the top of the bag, press the 10 cms turning towards the wrong side of the fabric. Sew them down through the centre with the matching thread. This seam neatens the end of the channel. Then along the top edge of the bag make a 4 cm double-folded hem to create a wide channel.

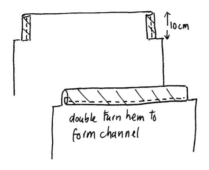

double turn hem to form channel

8 Place the two sides of the circle with right sides on the outside. With right sides together of the bag, and the bottom of the bag line up the raw edges together. The bag is a little bit bigger than the circle base so you need to put a couple of pleats in the seam under the pocket. Pin in place, sew with a 1 cm seam allowance and neaten with a zigzag stitch.

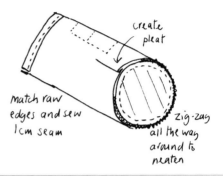

create pleat

match raw edges and sew 1cm seam

Zig-zag all the way around to neaten

6 With right sides together sew the side seam of the bag with a 15 mm seam allowance. Neaten both edges of the seam with zigzag stitch and create an open seam.

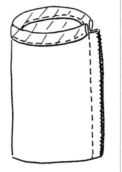

ROZ'S TIP

It is fun to make toggles and straps out of co-ordinating fabric rather than webbing.

9 Using a large safety pin attached to the rope, thread it through the channel then through one side of the toggle, then down through the 'D' ring and then back through the other side of the toggle. Next, tie the two ends of the rope together and manipulate the knot so it sits inside the channel.

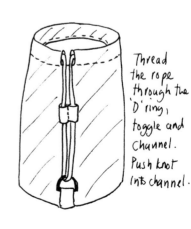

Thread the rope through the 'D' ring, toggle and channel. Push knot into channel.

7 Make the 'D ring tab and toggle by folding in half lengthwise and sewing a 1 cm seam. Turn through and press flat with the seam lying in the centre of one side. Thread the tab through the 'D' ring and sew in place at the bottom of the bag at the seam. Fold both ends of the toggle into the centre, then tuck the top fold under and sew down the middle securely.

thread 'D' ring through tab and sew to bottom of bag

Fold both ends inwards, tuck the outer end under and sew down the middle.

Creating two channels

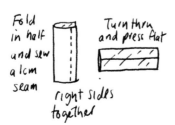

Fold in half and sew a 1cm seam

Turn thru and press flat

right sides together

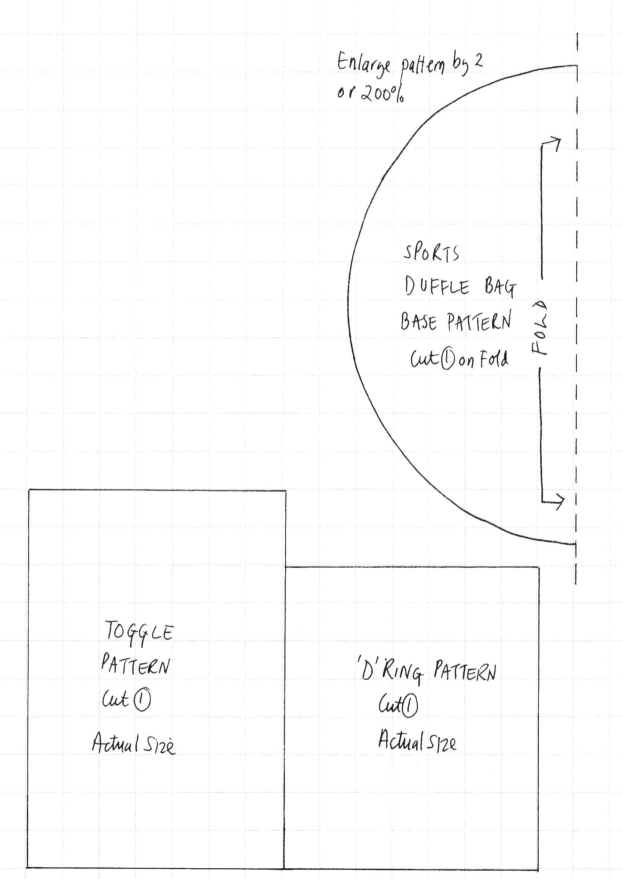

Enlarge pattern by 2
or 200%

SPORTS
DUFFLE BAG
BASE PATTERN
Cut ① on Fold

FOLD

TOGGLE
PATTERN
Cut ①

Actual Size

'D' RING PATTERN
Cut ①

Actual Size

OPULENT OCTOBER

Celebrating woodland creatures

THE MATERIALS YOU WILL NEED:

Mummy Owl
- 2 co-ordinating fat quarters for Mummy Ow
- 1 x 15 cms square of white felt for eyes
- 2 large buttons for eyes
- 1 x 30 cms square of orange felt for beak and feet
- Matching thread including white for eyes and orange for beak and feet

Baby Owl
- 2 co-ordinating fat quarters for Baby Owl
- 1 x 15 cms square of white felt for eyes
- 2 buttons for eyes
- 1 x 15 cms square of orange felt for beak and feet
- Matching thread including white for eyes and orange for beak and feet

Owl Family

My Owl Family was inspired by a lovely children's book I used to read to my girls when they were little. In fact my designs look nothing like the tawny owl drawings in the book but they do reflect the three babies sitting on a branch waiting for mummy owl to return from hunting.

CUTTING INSTRUCTIONS
HOW TO MAKE IT

1 **MUMMY OWL**
Enlarge the owl and wing pattern by two. Cut out the owl and wings out of the co-ordinating fabric.
BABY OWL
Copy the owl and wing pattern and cut them out of the co-ordinating fabric.

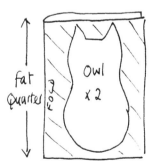

Copy out the corresponding eye, beak and feet pattern and cut out of felt.

2 **The Mummy Owl and Baby Owl are made in exactly the same way.**

Take the front of the owl, place on the white eyes pin and sew on with an edge stitch using matching thread. Place the beak beneath the eyes and sew in place with orange thread. Pick up the wings, place and sew with a zigzag stitch on the inside curve of the wing.

3 Sew on the buttons for eyes.

4 With right sides together sew the owl shape together using a 1 cm seam allowance and leaving a gap at the bottom for the stuffing. Snip curves and excess material off the top of the ears.

5 Turn the owl through and stuff. Make sure you stuff up into the ears first and then the tummy. When fully stuffed, sew up the gap with a slip stitch. Make the feet by sewing two together with an edge stitch using orange thread. Then handsew the feet onto the bottom of the owl.

Mummy Owl is longer and thinner than baby owl so she needs to be enlarged by 2 or 200%.

Actual size for beak and foot and
                                    eye

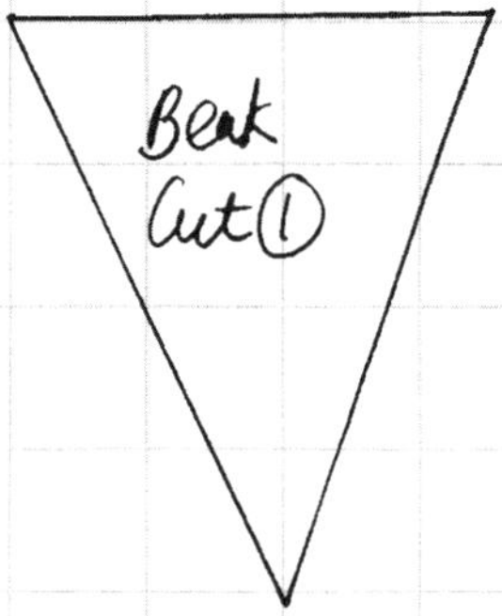

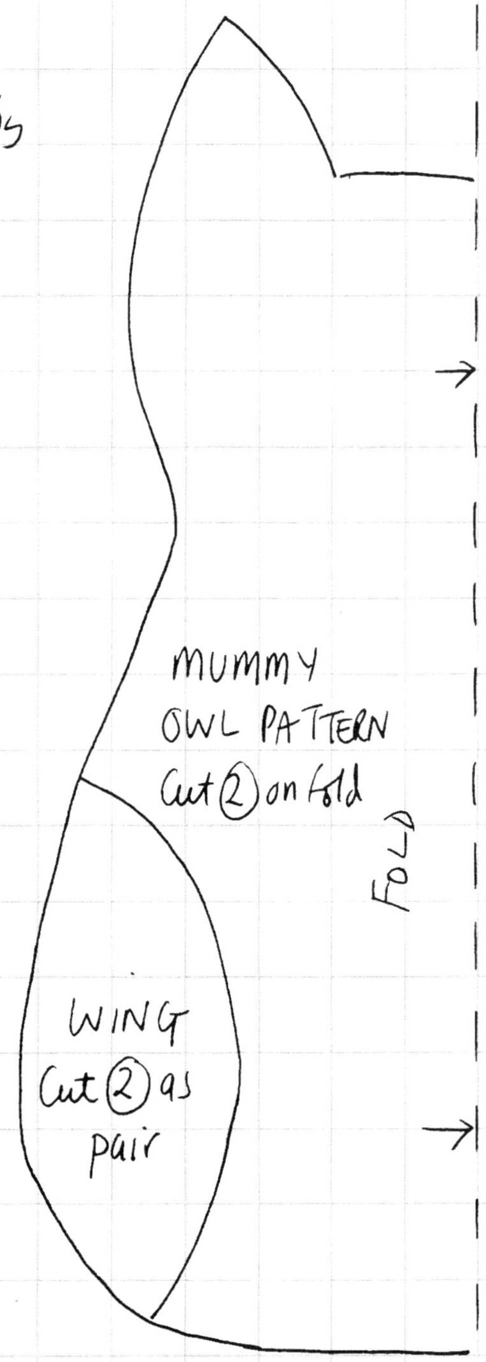

Beak
Cut ①

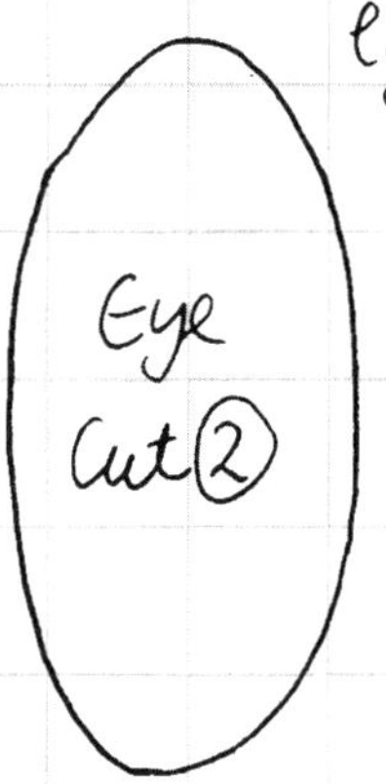

Eye
Cut ②

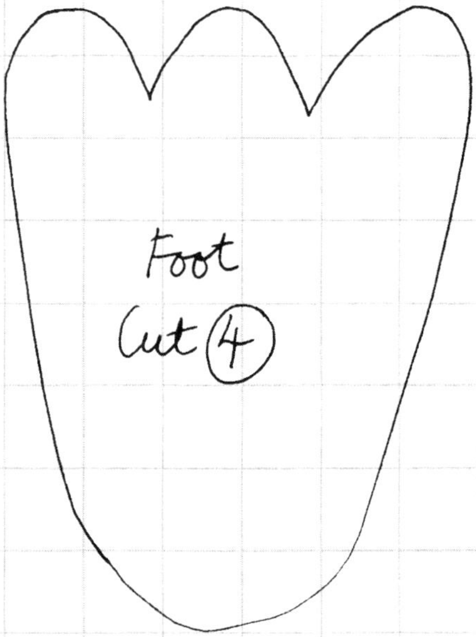

MUMMY
OWL PATTERN
Cut ② on fold

FOLD

Foot
Cut ④

WING
Cut ② as
pair

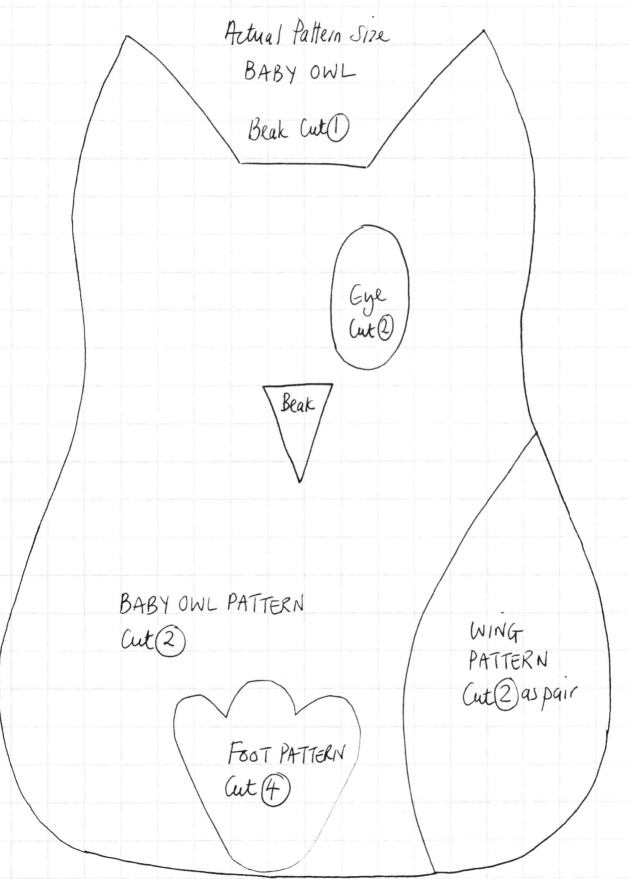

Actual Pattern Size
BABY OWL

Beak Cut ①

Eye
Cut ②

Beak

BABY OWL PATTERN
Cut ②

FOOT PATTERN
Cut ④

WING
PATTERN
Cut ② as pair

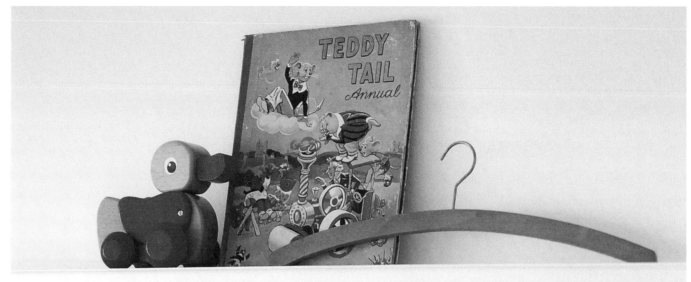

THE MATERIALS
YOU WILL NEED:

- 0.70 m of Calico
- 3 x 30 cms co-ordinating felt squares for pockets
- 1 x 30 cms square of orange felt for the fox
- 1 x 30 cms square of dark brown felt for the hedgehog
- 1 x 30 cms square of dark grey felt for the badger
- 3 x 15 cm squares of felt in white, brown and black
- 4 x 50 cms of ribbon for tying
- Matching threads: orange, brown, grey, white, black and the colour of the pockets

Hanging Pockets

This project provides you with a creative way to keep shoes neat and tidy using skills you have already acquired. The same idea can be applied to other areas in the house where you need simple storage solutions.

CUTTING INSTRUCTIONS
HOW TO MAKE IT

To keep ribbon ties strong, cut double the length you want the tie to be and then catch in the folded end into your sewing.

1. Cut out a rectangle of calico, 76 cm x 66 cm. Cut out three pockets 30 cms x 21 cm. Copy out the actual size animal patterns and cut out of felt as suggested.

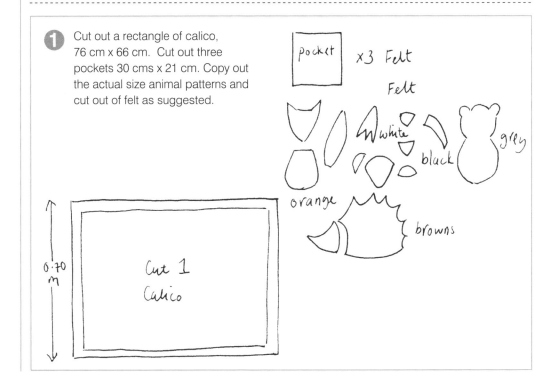

2 **Decorate each pocket with an animal:**
Fox

Hand sew the eyes with a satin stitch in black thread. To ensure the shape and positioning is correct, draw the eye on the wrong side of the fox first. Position the fox onto the pocket and sew on the body with the head over the top and the tail tucked in underneath. Sew on with an edge stitch. Then place the cheeks and tail tip and sew on with an edge stitch followed by the nose.

Hedgehog

Hand sew the eye with a satin stitch with black thread. To ensure the shape and positioning is correct, draw the eye on the wrong side of the hedgehog first. Position the hedgehog onto the pocket and sew on the body with the head over the top. Sew on with an edge stitch and finally sew on the nose.

Badger

Hand sew the eyes with a satin stitch with a white thread onto the black stripes of the badger's face. Position the badger onto the pocket and sew on the body with an edge stitch. Place the head over the top and stitch in place and then finally sew the stripes and the nose. Use an edge stitch throughout.

3 To give the pockets a little depth, sew in two pleats along the bottom edge 5 cm from each outside edge.

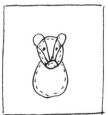

4 Centralise the three pockets along the 76 cm side leaving a gap of 3 cm in-between the pockets and 27.5 cm from the top. The right sides should be facing one another and the pocket should be dropping down. Sew this seam 30 cm from the edge of the pocket. Then flip the pocket up, so the right side shows, make sure the side seams of the pockets are at right angles to the bottom line and sew in place with an edge stitch.

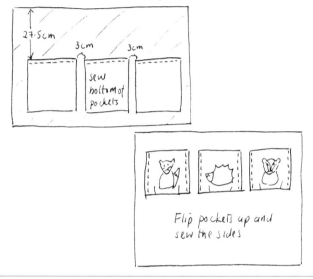

5 Once all the pockets are sewn on, fold the calico in two over the pockets and even with the top edge. Sew the side seams with a 1 cm seam allowance. Snip the corners and turn through.

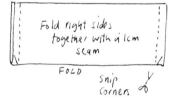

6 At the top opening, tuck in a 3 cm turning and iron in place. Fold each ribbon in half and distribute evenly along the top edge, place inside the turning and pin in position. Sew this top edge together with two rows of stitching, 2 cm apart. This should make the pockets strong enough to carry all sorts of bits and pieces.

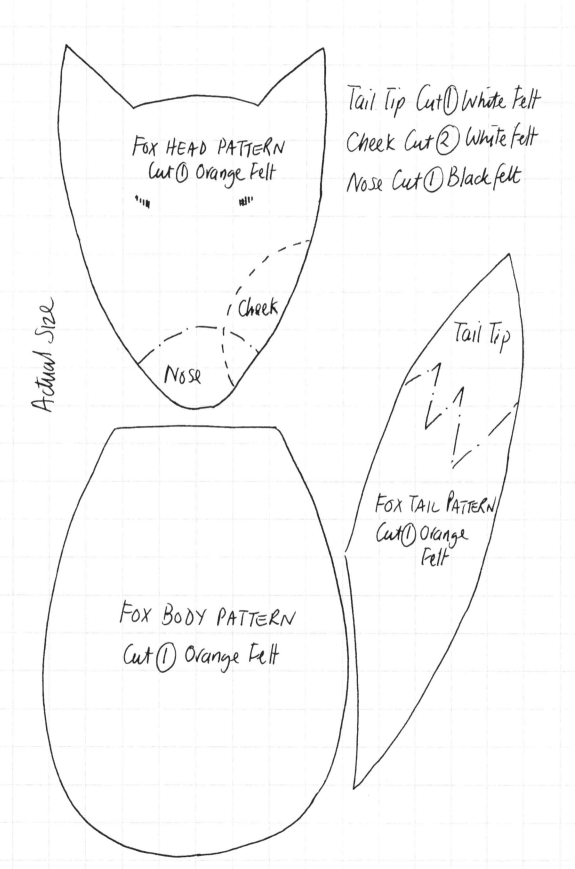

Tail Tip Cut ① White Felt
Cheek Cut ② White Felt
Nose Cut ① Black Felt

Fox HEAD PATTERN
Cut ① Orange Felt

Actual Size

Cheek

Nose

Tail Tip

Fox TAIL PATTERN
Cut ① Orange Felt

Fox BODY PATTERN
Cut ① Orange Felt

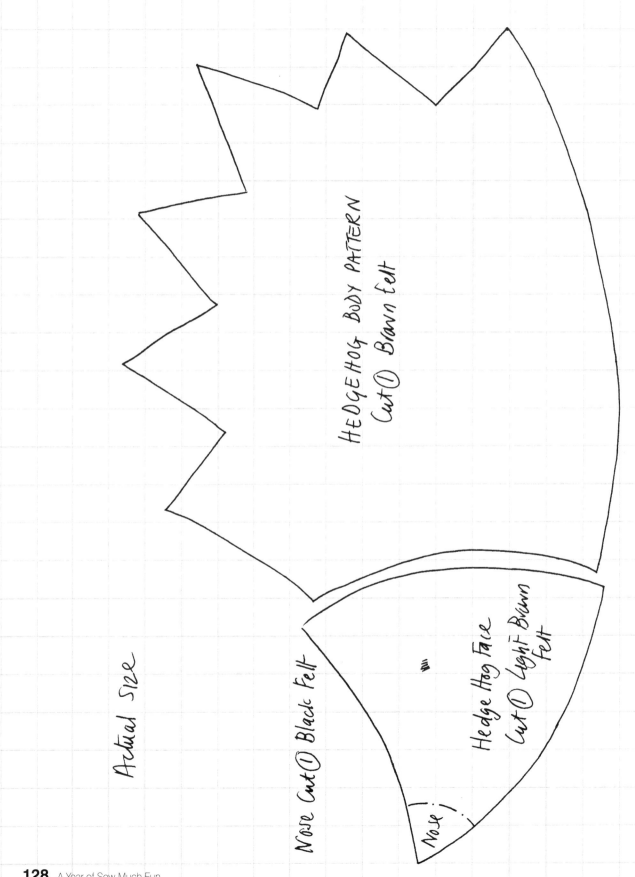

Actual Size

HEDGEHOG BODY PATTERN
Cut(1) Brown Felt

Nose Cut(1) Black Felt

Hedge Hog Face
Cut(1) Light Brown Felt

Nose

Actual Size

Eye Stripe Pattern Cut ② Black Felt
Nose Pattern Cut ① Black Felt

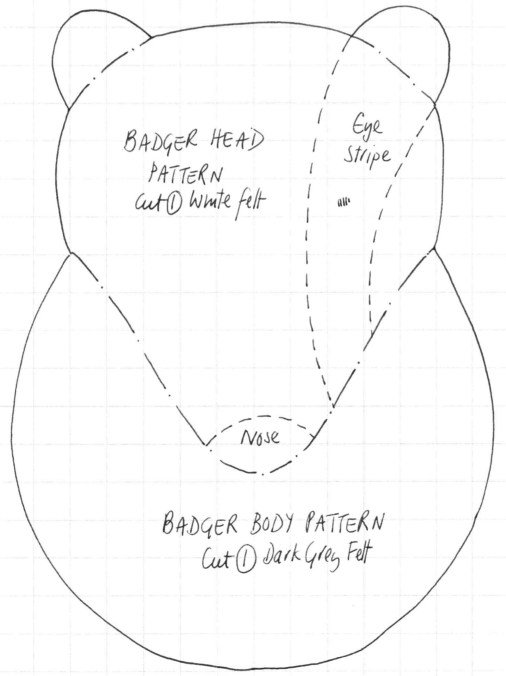

BADGER HEAD
PATTERN
Cut ① White felt

Eye
Stripe

Nose

BADGER BODY PATTERN
Cut ① Dark Grey Felt

NUMBING NOVEMBER

Time to get cosy

THE MATERIALS
YOU WILL NEED:

Russian Doll Scarf

- 0.25 m fleece
- 2 x 15 cm washable felt squares for the main two colours of the Russian Doll dress
- Scraps of pink and brown felt for the face and hair
- 1 x 15 cms of white lace trim
- 1 x 15 cms of white daisy trim
- 1 x rose trim
- Matching thread and red and brown thread for face

Soldier Scarf

- 0.25 m fleece
- 2 x 15 cm washable felt squares of red and black

Scraps of pink and white felt for the face and uniform

- Matching thread and black thread for the eyes

Scarf

Do you need to persuade your little one to keep their scarf on in the cold? Then make them one with their favourite character or creature on it!

CUTTING INSTRUCTIONS
HOW TO MAKE IT

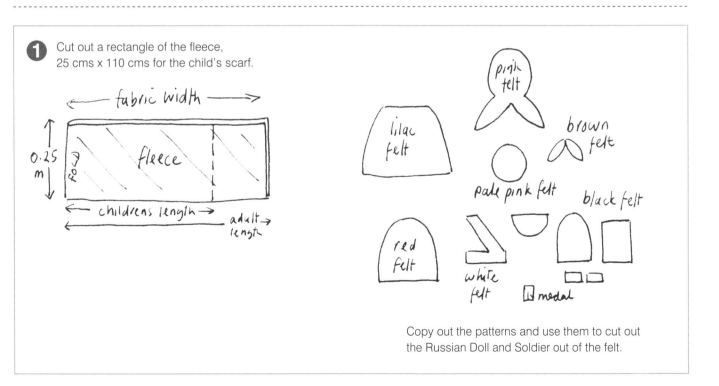

1 Cut out a rectangle of the fleece,
25 cms x 110 cms for the child's scarf.

fabric width

0.25 m

fleece

childrens length

adult length

pink felt

lilac felt

brown felt

pale pink felt

black felt

red felt

white felt

medal

Copy out the patterns and use them to cut out the Russian Doll and Soldier out of the felt.

2 Decorate the Russian Doll scarf
Hand sew the eyes on the face with a satin stitch and a little 'V' stitch for the mouth. Then sew the face and hair onto the headscarf using an edge stitch.

3 Sew the white trim onto the dolls skirt using an edge stitch and place the dolls skirt in the middle of the scarf around 15 cms up from the bottom. Sew the dolls skirt onto the scarf using an edge stitch. Then place the headscarf over the skirt and sew in place using an edge stitch. Finish off by sewing on a rose by hand in the middle of the headscarf above the skirt.

Never iron fleece – it ruins the fluffy texture. If you get creases in it just give it a good wash.

4 Decorate the Soldier scarf
Sew the eyes on the face using a back stitch. Sew the white trim onto the body. Place the legs of the soldier in the middle of the scarf around 15 cms up from the bottom and sew onto the scarf. Then place the jacket on top of the legs and sew in place catching in the cuffs. Then repeat for the head and the hat.

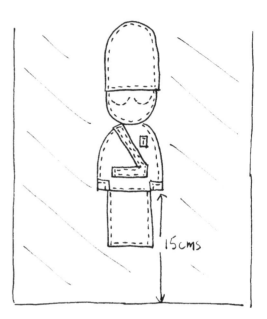

5 Neaten the scarf edge by sewing a single-folded hem all the way around.

This scarf can have any design sewn on it but these are a couple of my favourite characters which often appear on our popular 'comfort cushion kits'.

To make an adult-sized scarf just cut the fleece 30 cms x 150 cms.

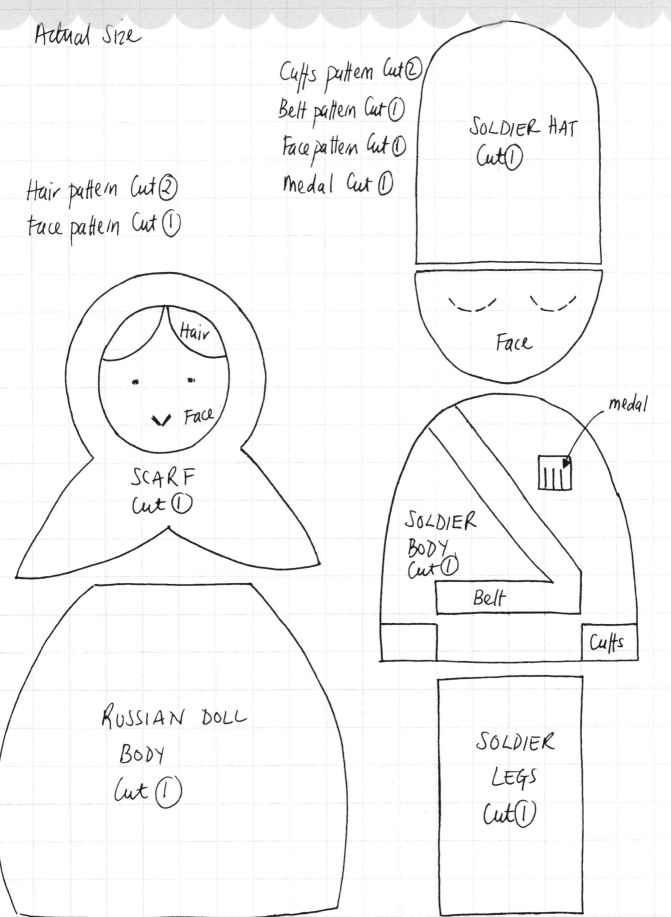

Actual Size

Cuffs pattern Cut ②
Belt pattern Cut ①
Face pattern Cut ①
Medal Cut ①

SOLDIER HAT
Cut ①

Hair pattern Cut ②
Face pattern Cut ①

Hair

Face

Face

SCARF
Cut ①

medal

SOLDIER
BODY
Cut ①

Belt

Cuffs

RUSSIAN DOLL
BODY
Cut ①

SOLDIER
LEGS
Cut ①

THE MATERIALS YOU WILL NEED:

- 0.30 m fleece colour 1
- 0.30 m fleece colour 2
- 0.30 m fleece colour 3
- 0.30 m fleece colour 4
- 0.30 m fleece colour 5
- 1.50 m of backing fabric, 150 cms wide
- 4 x 30 cms felt squares in pink, grey, green and blue.
- 5 x 15 cms felt squares in pale pink, dark blue, bright yellow, egg yellow, light green and the colour of the elephant's saddle.
- 30 cm pink Ric-Rac trim for the Flamingo, 20 cm Ric-Rac to match the elephant's saddle
- 15 cms green Ric-Rac for the turtle
- Matching thread for the felt and fleece
- 1 safety pin

Blanket

With this blanket we combine some of Sew Much Fun's favourite hand sewing designs to decorate a large patchwork blanket made out of many colours of fleece. The challenge for this project is completing an even larger project – it gets heavy, unwieldy and awkward but you get a feeling of great satisfaction when the last stitch is sewn.

CUTTING INSTRUCTIONS
HOW TO MAKE IT

1 Cut out 5 x 28 cm squares in each of the fleece colours. Copy the animal patterns and cut out of felt. Cut a backing piece approximately 1.40 m x 1.40 m square.

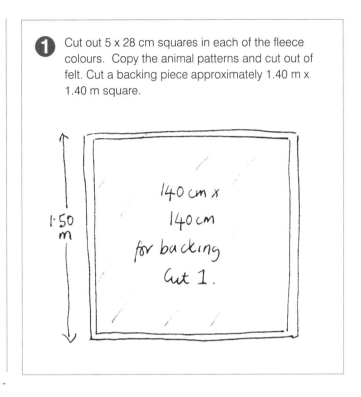

2 **Take one square from each colour of fleece and appliqué with one of the animals.**

Hand sew all the eyes on with a satin stitch and the mouths with a backstitch. The patterns show the correct position which you can copy onto the wrong side of the animal with a pencil to use as a guide. Sew Ric-Rac on the elephant's saddle and the turtle's shell and use it for the flamingo's legs.
Sew all the animals to the fleece using an edge stitch.

hand stitch face, trim shell and edge stitch appliqué

hand stitch eye, Trim saddle and edge stitch appliqué

hand stitch face, edgestitch appliqué.

hand stitch face and edge stitch appliqué

hand stitch eye, sew on legs edge stitch appliqué

3 Choose the order in which you want to sew your five rows of five squares together. Then sewing your right sides together, join your squares in strips using a foot width seam allowance. Then taking your five strips, sew them right sides together again with a foot width seam allowance. You cannot press fleece so you just have to keep the seams flat when you are sewing them together.

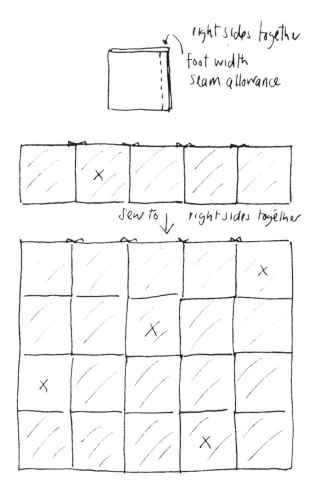

right sides together
foot width seam allowance

Sew to → right sides together

4 Taking the patchwork side uppermost and your cotton backing on top, place your right sides together. Smoothing out all layers from the centre, safety pin together from the middle outwards. Pin around the edge and sew from the fleece side using a 1 cm seam allowance and leaving a gap to turn through.

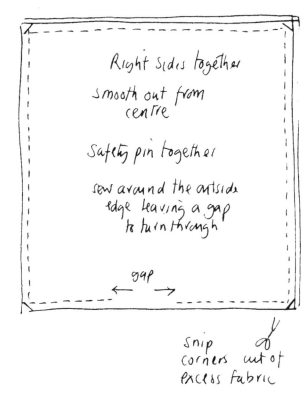

Right Sides together

smooth out from centre

Safety pin together

sew around the outside edge leaving a gap to turn through

gap

snip corners out of excess fabric

5 Unpin, cut off excess fabric, snip corners and turn through so you can lay out flat. To help keep it flat at the edges and sew up the gap, sew a top stitch row through both layers all the way around the blanket.

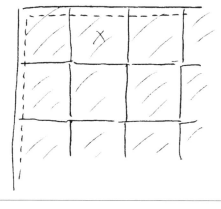

ROZ'S TIP

If you cut out two sides of the animal templates you can just hand sew little animals. All of these creatures are popular in our hand sewing classes.

Actual Size

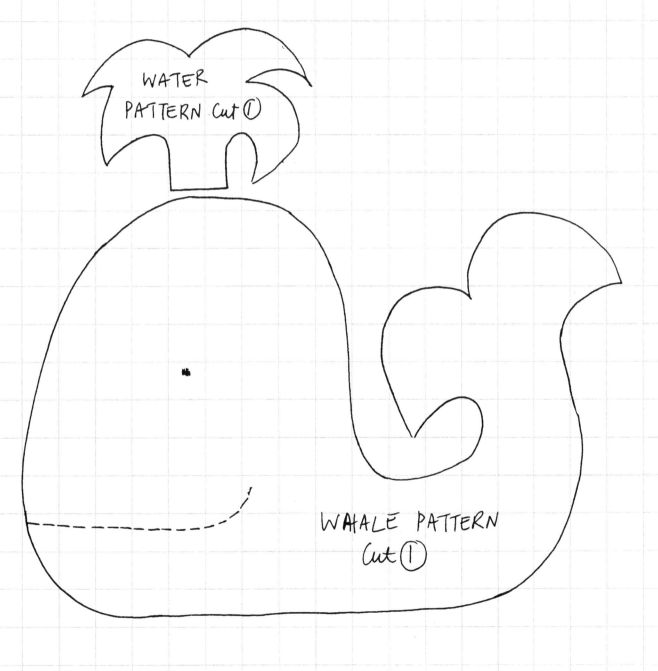

WATER
PATTERN Cut ①

WHALE PATTERN
Cut ①

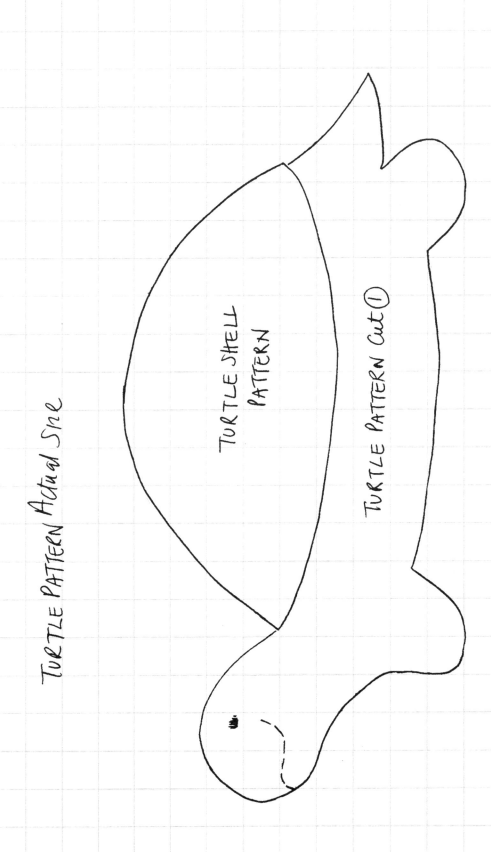

TURTLE PATTERN Actual Size

TURTLE SHELL PATTERN

TURTLE PATTERN Cut ①

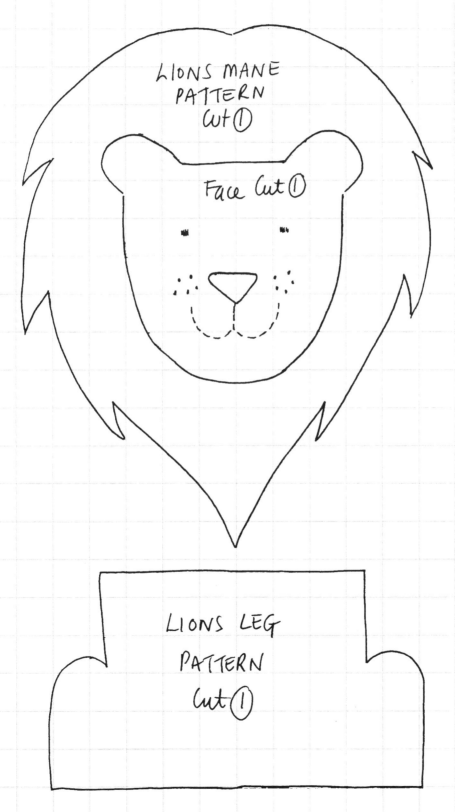

Actual Size

LIONS MANE
PATTERN
Cut ①

Face Cut ①

LIONS LEG
PATTERN
Cut ①

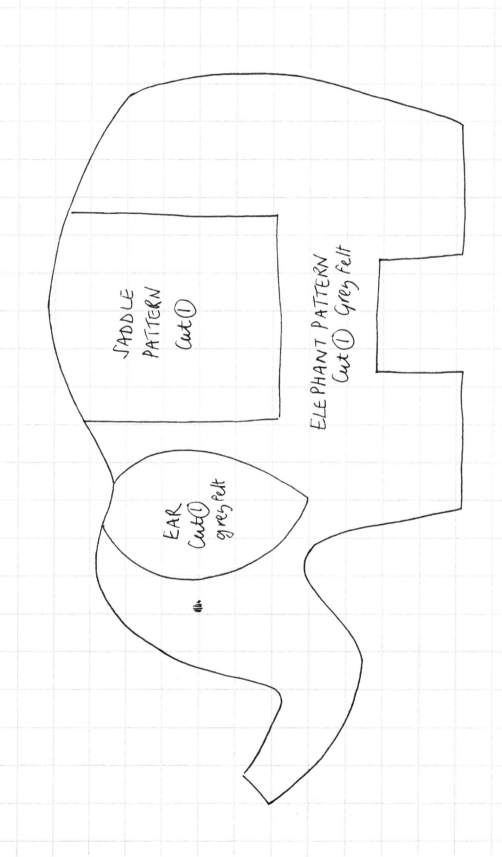

ELE PHANT PATTERN Actual Size

SADDLE PATTERN Cut ①

EAR Cut① grey Felt

ELE PHANT PATTERN Cut① Grey Felt

Actual Size

FLAMINGO
PATTERN
Cut ①

Beak

BEAK PATTERN
Cut ①

WING
PATTERN
Cut ①

DECORATIVE DECEMBER

Christmas essentials

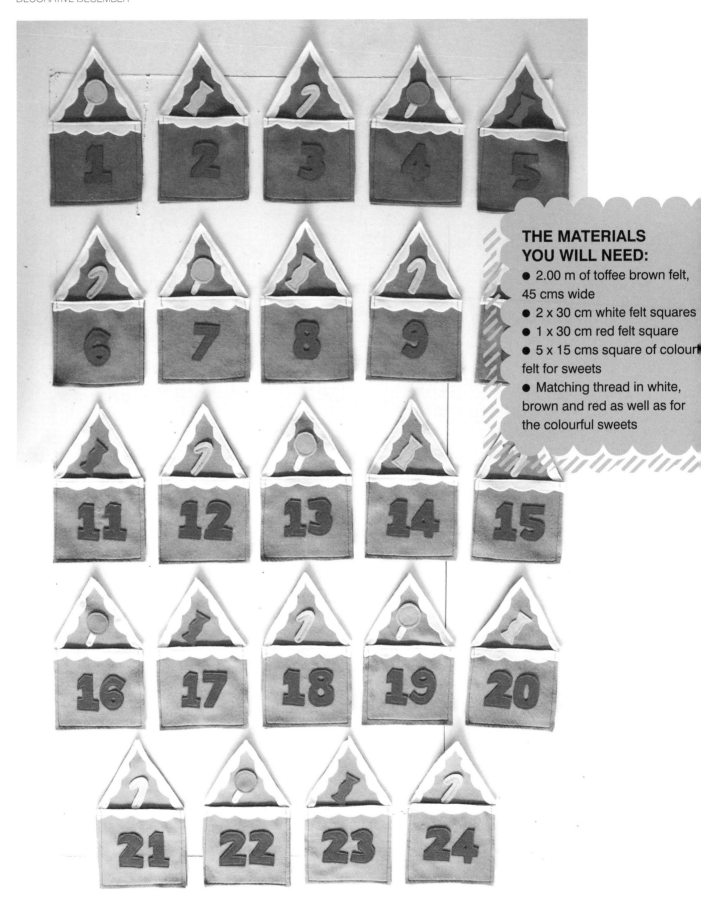

THE MATERIALS YOU WILL NEED:
- 2.00 m of toffee brown felt, 45 cms wide
- 2 x 30 cm white felt squares
- 1 x 30 cm red felt square
- 5 x 15 cms square of colour felt for sweets
- Matching thread in white, brown and red as well as for the colourful sweets

Gingerbread House Advent Calender

These Gingerbread Houses can either be pegged up in a row or scattered all over the house with little gifts stored in their pouches. This is a repetitive project but I can assure you that by the end, your accurate sewing machine skills will be magnificent!

CUTTING INSTRUCTIONS
HOW TO MAKE IT

1 Copy the pattern for the gingerbread house, pocket, snow, numbers and sweets. Using the toffee brown felt cut out 24 of the houses and pockets. Using the white felt cut out the three snow strips 24 times. With the red felt cut out enough number combinations to get you to 24! Use all the other colours to give you a variety of 24 sweets.

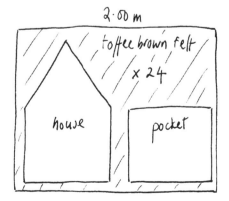

2 **It is best to make these advent houses one process at a time across all 24 houses, as you will need to repeat each process 24 times!**

Take the pocket piece and place the advent number (or numbers) in the middle 3 cms down from the top. Sew on using an edge stitch with a matching red thread.

3 Sew on the snow trim onto the top edge of the pocket and onto the apex of the house.

4 Place the sweet at an angle in the middle of the house apex and sew on with an edge stitch or just straight down the middle in a matching coloured thread.

5 The final process is to sew on the pocket to the gingerbread house using a foot width as your seam allowance to make sure you don't get any holes.

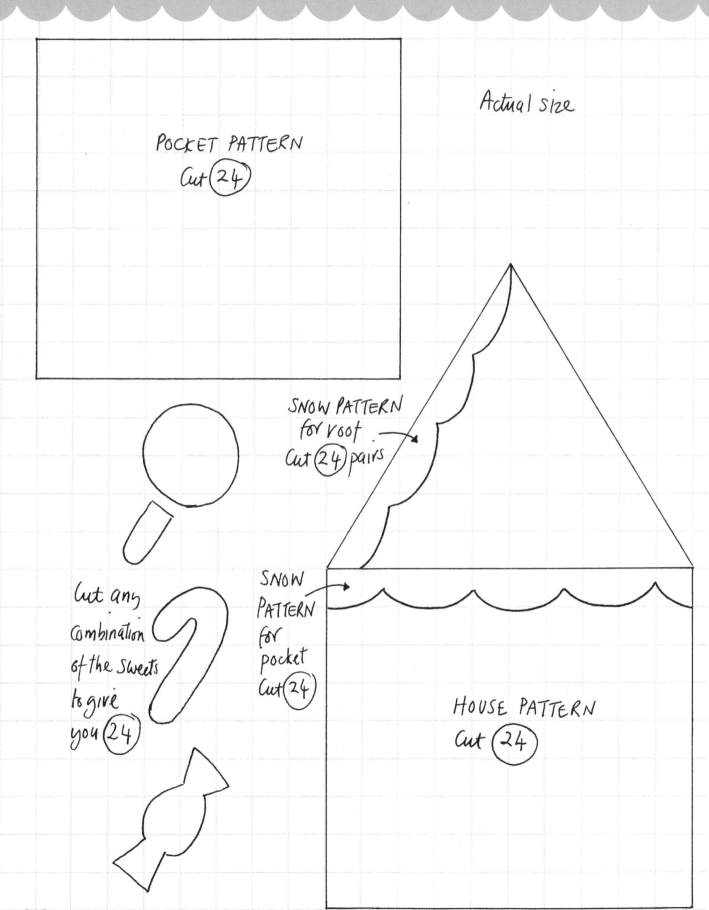

Actual size

POCKET PATTERN
Cut (24)

SNOW PATTERN
for roof
Cut (24) pairs

SNOW
PATTERN
for
pocket
Cut (24)

Cut any
combination
of the sweets
to give
you (24)

HOUSE PATTERN
Cut (24)

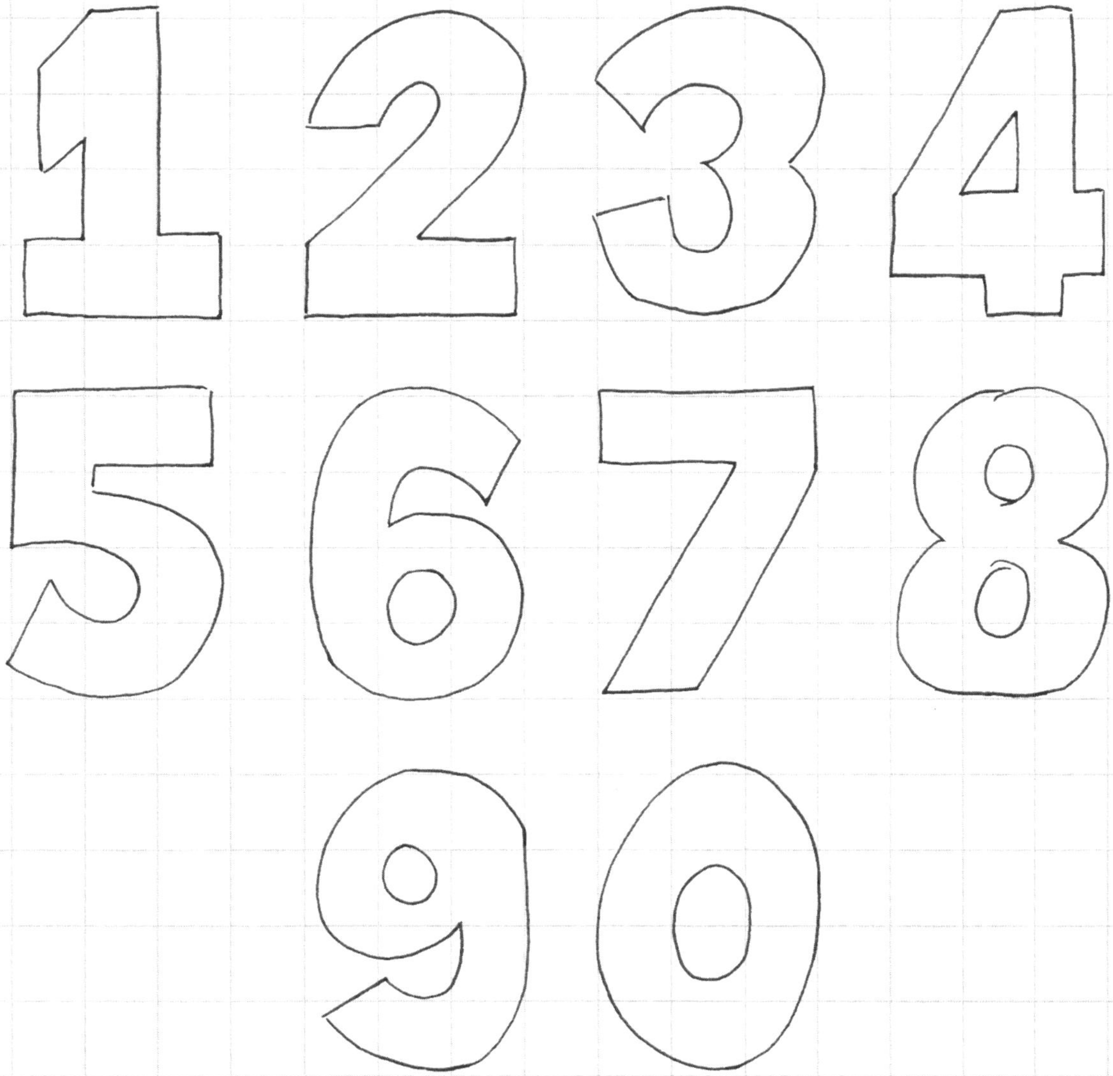

1 2 3 4
5 6 7 8
9 0

Actual size number patterns
drawn by hand for a hand crafted feel!

THE MATERIALS YOU WILL NEED:
(To make two stockings)

- 0.50 m of red fleece
- 0.50 m of cream fleece
- 1 fat quarter of co-ordinating red gingham
- 0.25 m of interlining
- Red embroidery thread
- Matching thread

Simple Stockings

Our stockings are infamous and can be made in many colours with names and initials embroidered onto the gingham hearts but here we have kept it simple. You can either keep them small or increase this perfect shape to your preferred size.

CUTTING INSTRUCTIONS
HOW TO MAKE IT

1 Enlarge the stocking pattern by two. Copy the heart pattern on the fold. Cut out a pair of stockings making sure the stretch of the fleece goes across the width way of the stocking not the length.

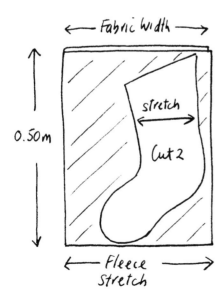

Prepare the gingham fabric with a square of interlining (large enough for the heart pattern), ironed onto the wrong side of the fabric. Then cut out the heart shape.

Cut out a rectangle 6 cm x 30cm out of the gingham for the stocking hanger.

2 Take one side of your stocking and place the heart 15 cm down from the top and in the middle of the stocking. Pin in place. Using embroidery thread sew on the heart using an over stitch.

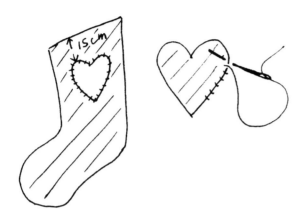

4 Make the stocking hanger by ironing the rectangle in two lengthwise, and then the two long sides into the centre fold. Sew in place.

5 Along the top of the stocking make a 1 cm single fold and sew in place. Then attach the stocking hanger to the top, tucking the ends under and sewing in place.

3 Place the right sides together and sew around the stocking with a 1 cm seam allowance. Snip in around the curves.

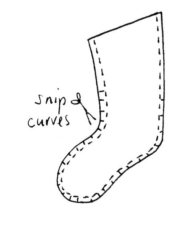

ROZ'S TIP *When cutting out fleece always consider where the stretch is as your project will naturally stretch in that direction.*

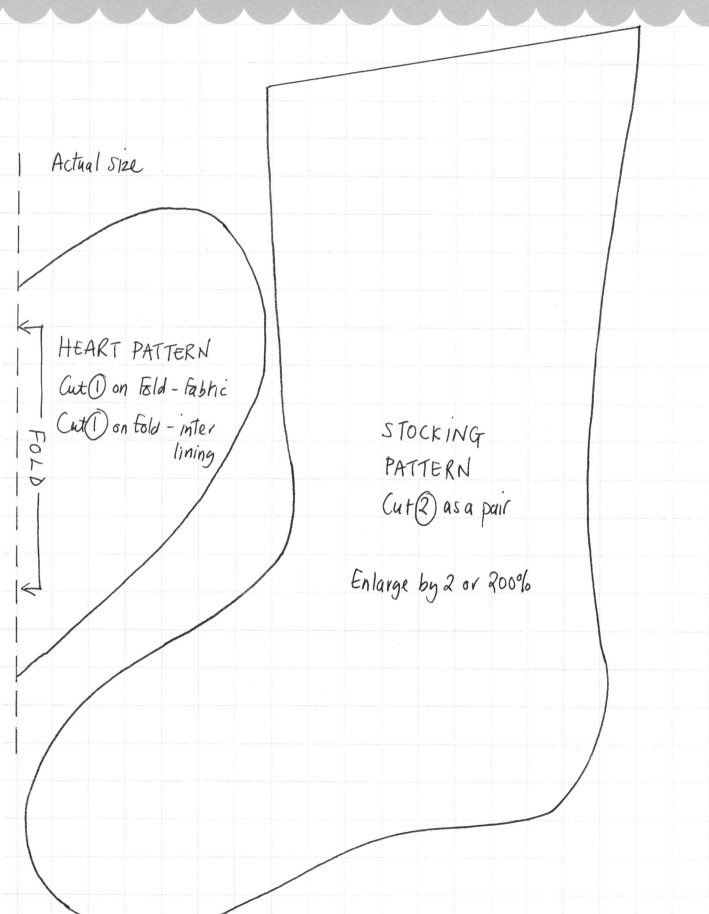

Actual size

HEART PATTERN
Cut ① on Fold - Fabric
Cut ① on fold - inter
         lining

FOLD

STOCKING
PATTERN
Cut ② as a pair

Enlarge by 2 or 200%

SEWING TECHNIQUES

There are many sewing techniques but in this chapter I will only describe the ones you need for the projects in this book.

HAND SEWING

Preparing your needle and thread

Always cut your thread with sharp scissors and thread it through the eye of the needle. To start with, an embroidery needle is best as the eye is large. If working with children make a double thread by drawing both threads to the same length. If not then draw the thread out from the needle about a third of the way down.

thread through needle and draw to a similar length

Tying a knot

at the end of the thread create a loop then thread the needle through the loop a knot will form. Repeat.

Casting on and off

I often don't use a knot because sometimes it is not secure. For better security at the beginning and end of your sewing, sew a few little stitches.

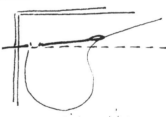

a few little stitches on top of one another 'Casting on' and 'casting off'

Running Stitch

when you are younger just do one stitch at a time remembering 'up to the sky' and 'down to the ground'

Back stitch

⑤

Satin Stitch

⑥

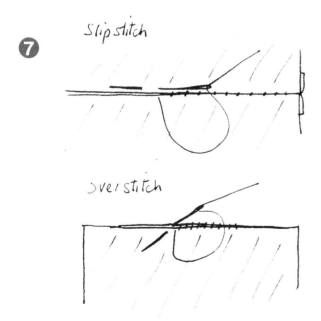

several long
stitches
side by
side
to create an
eye shape

Slip Stitch or Over Stitch

A slip stitch is the neater way of sewing up a gap in your machine sewing but it is hard to get used to slipping your thread under the fold of the fabric and then repeating the other side. If you find this difficult, return to an overstitch where you do a diagonal stitch across the two openings. For both methods keep your stitches small and even.

⑦ Slip stitch

over stitch

Sewing on a button

Using a double thread, knot one end and sew at least five stitches and then cast off on the wrong side of the fabric.

⑧

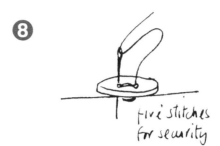

five stitches
for security

KEY TO ALL MY ILLUSTRATIONS
In all my sketches I have shaded the right side of the outer fabric with lines unless it is felt or lining fabric.

wrong side   right side

right side

MACHINE SEWING
Straight Stitch
Most of the time you will be sewing your seams with a straight stitch.

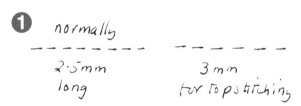

Zigzag Stitch
This stitch is mainly used for neatening off raw edges of your fabric so they can withstand washing or for sewing on your appliqué designs. For stitching with knitted fabrics, make a shallow zigzag stitch which will help with the stretch and also be easy to unpick if you make a mistake!

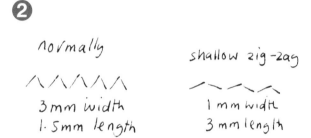

Back stitch
As you sew your seam, back stitch at the beginning and end of any construction seam to secure your stitching.

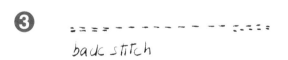

SEAMS
A seam is when you join two pieces of fabric with right sides together to make a project. They can be straight, curved or have a corner. For more accuracy, draw a line along the seam on the wrong side of the fabric at the correct seam allowance from the edge with some tailor's chalk.

Open and closed seams
Most seams are either open or closed. If it is an open seam then both raw edges are zigzagged separately and the seam turning is pressed flat. If it is a closed seam the raw edges are zigzagged together and the seam turning is pressed to one side.

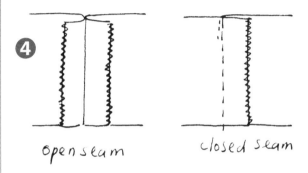

Single Fold and Double Fold Hems
You always have to consider how you will neaten the hem of your project and a double fold is often the solution. This technique is also used to make channels for elastic and drawstrings.

Turn your fabric to the wrong side by 1 cm and then again by the amount you need to make the hem.

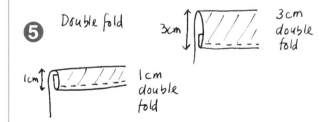

A single fold hem is just turning your fabric up once and can only really be used like this when sewing with a fabric that does not fray.

Seams need to be snipped before they get turned through.

6

snip along curve

snip to release corner

snip of excess fabric

Topstitching, edge stitching and zigzag appliqué

These are mainly aesthetic decisions which give you a neat finish.

7 Edge stitching

Top stitching

Zig-Zag stitch overlapping appliqué edge

Threading elastic through a channel

Thread the elastic through the channel using a safety pin.

8 Threading through elastic/cord along a channel

Thread through with safety pin

Pin to secure one end

2cm elastic overlap and sew

5mm elastic tie a knot

CUTTING AND FABRIC

It is essential to have a brief understanding of fabric to enable you to cut out your patterns correctly.

Fabric is purchased by the metre or part metre, measured along the selvedge edge and will vary in width from 110 cms to 150 cms. You can also buy fabric in a fat quarter which is 50 cms x 55 cms and is a very economical way to get a range of fabric print.

- **'Selvedge' edge** – is formed along the lengthwise edge of the fabric – it does not fray
- **'Warp' threads** – run along the length of the fabric and tend to be the stronger thread
- **'Weft' threads** – run from the left to right of the fabric
- **'Grainline'** – is parallel to the 'selvedge'
- **Bias'** – is at a 45 degree angle to the warp and weft

The knitted fabric is treated the same way for the projects in this book.

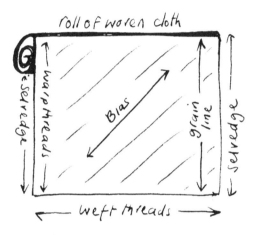

To cut patterns out correctly you keep them in line with the warp and weft threads unless you are cutting on the bias. Lay your fabric flat on the table, or if required make a fold parallel to the selvedge edge. Always check for fabrics with a one-way design and make sure you cut the design in the right direction.

Pin on your pattern following the instructions and cut out using your sharp fabric scissors. Keep one of the scissor blades resting on the table and cut with a full blade giving you a nice straight line. Don't over pin your pattern on, a pin every 8-10 cms should be fine.

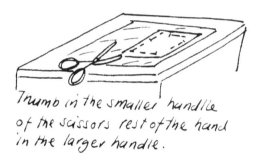

Thumb in the smaller handle of the scissors rest of the hand in the larger handle.

If you are cutting straight squares for patchwork or triangles for bunting and you are a responsible adult you can try using a rotary knife, cutting mat and ruler. Place your fabric flat onto the table, no more than two thicknesses deep. Use the lines on the mat and ruler to guide your cut and hold your ruler firmly whilst releasing the safety catch on the rotary blade and cut away from yourself.

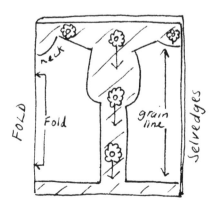

You want the flowers to grow up the top.

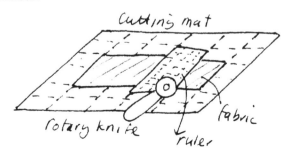

PATTERNS

When sewing it is always wise to use patterns to cut out your shapes. This gives you a chance to build up a library of patterns that you can use again and again and also avoids you making mistakes when cutting out.

In this book we provide patterns or pattern measurements for each project so you can make your own patterns. We recommend that you use pattern paper but you can use tracing paper. You can also use a photocopier to copy or enlarge the patterns or you can enlarge them yourself as shown below.

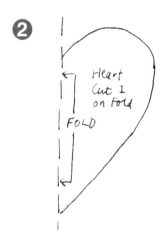

A pattern is often symmetrical so we tend to cut it out on a fold. To identify this on the pattern there will be a long bracket with the word 'fold'. It is also important to identify the name of the pattern, the size and how many times you need to cut it out and which materials you need to cut it out of.

Patterns also have other markings to show the 'grainline', 'notches' and 'decoration markings'. All of this helps you to cut out and sew the project correctly.

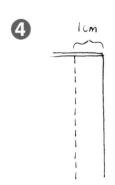

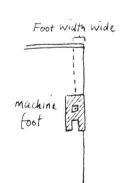

All the patterns in this book include seam allowances where necessary. A seam allowance is the width between the cut edge of the pattern and the sewing line. They vary from a foot width wide to 1 cm.

MEASUREMENTS

When you start to make clothes for your family and friends it is useful to take some key measurements listed below. It is important to remember that a baby's head is large in comparison to its size and the circumference does not increase in proportion to the body. Also the chest, waist and hip measurement does not grow at the same rate as height so that is why dresses for 2/3 year olds can often become successful tops for 5/6 year olds.

- Height
- Head circumference
- Neck circumference
- Chest/Bust circumference
- Waist circumference
- Hip (widest point) circumference
- Front Rise
- Back Rise
- Inside leg length
- Waist to knee length
- Sleeve Length

As requested by my students here is a diagram showing where you take those measurements from. The same is similar for adults. A useful extra circumference measurement is 'where you like to wear an elasticated waist' which is a personal preference but should be somewhere between the waist and hip.

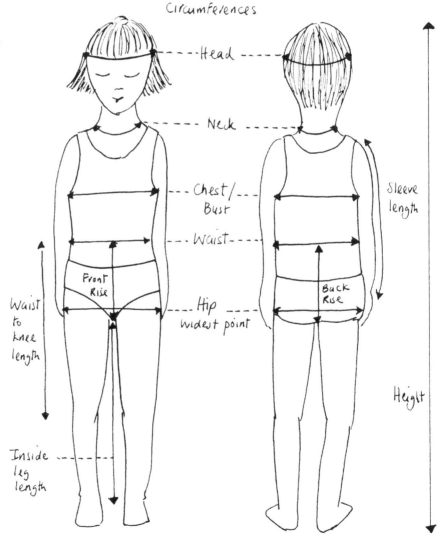

For girls, boys and adults.

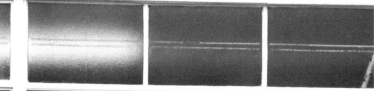

Sew Much Fun
Victoria Gardens
Victoria Street
Windermere
LA23 1AD
Cumbria

015394 48852

Sew Much Fun
46 Chalcot Road
Primrose Hill
London
NW1 8LS

0207 722 9889

www.sewmuchfun.co.uk

"Roz has taught me that with enough fabric and time I can rule the world with all my awesome ideas."
EMILY, aged 14

Acknowledgements

I would like to start off by thanking Alistair from House of Alistair who encouraged me to write this Sew Much Fun book but advised me that the traditional publishing route might not suit me! My solution was to self-publish giving me the opportunity to surround myself with a small but experienced team. Thank you to Emily for providing the discipline and editorial advice and keeping us all on track, Margarita for the photographic styling and the beautiful book design and Piero for his calm and gentle approach to the photography. Miles from Choir publishing also needs a mention for his patience in bringing this publication to fruition.

I also need to thank my family who have all contributed in their own ways. Thank you Mummy for your contribution to the chapter titles, Florence for your tremendous help in making the sample projects, Georgia for the essential help in completing the odd sample here and there and of course to Geoffrey who somehow supports all my creative exploits however time consuming they might be.

Thank you to my students who have tried and tested many of these projects over the years and have inspired me to write them down so many others can share 'Sew Much Fun'.

Last but not least a big thank you to everyone who works at Sew Much Fun for passing on my enthusiasm for creative sewing.

This quilt is made from some of the fabric pieces left over from making every project in the book! Creative sewing just goes on forever.

"I was hoping to be able to make a few cushions at first but with Roz's encouragement and teaching I have made some fairly complex dresses, tops and skirts! Although I live in Enfield I keep coming back. Sew Much Fun is an oasis of calm in busy London where you know you will get a warm welcome, get creative, meet amazing people and leave wearing something new!" LEIGH

"I love the red spider I made at Sew Much Fun – it was my idea and Roz helped me make it. I love the materials that I chose and it is more fun playing with something I made myself." RAFFERTY, 5 years old

"I can honestly say the children are never happier than when they are at Sew Much Fun. It is an inspirational place where children experience the simple joy and sense of achievement of making something with their own hands." KIKI

"Roz's teaching approach is very, very positive. There is a lot of fun and laughter in her classes and we benefit from her incredible knowledge and experience. Roz is a professional with a huge passion for her subject. She has a solution to every sewing problem one comes across." ANNE

"Every Wednesday I turn up with my bag full of fabric, pins and needles and random ideas which I throw at Roz and she helps me turn odd scraps into beautiful little clothes for my grandchildren and occasionally something for myself. It is wonderful to indulge my passion with likeminded people." JENNY

"My favourite thing I've made at Sew Much Fun is a ballet bag. Roz helped me make a pair of ballet shoes with ribbons and roses to sew on the outside. It is very pretty and I love taking it to my ballet class!" KAI, 9 years old

"Sew Much Fun is unique because in any one class you might be sitting next to someone who is sewing a cushion and another person who is sewing an evening gown. Roz makes everyone very welcome – any age and any level." REBECCA